ANGELS, GHOSTS AND DEMONS

Erica Gammon

Raven Crest Books

Published by: Raven Crest Books
www.ravencrestbooks.com

ISBN-13: 978-0-9934439-3-0

FOREWORD

Hello again Reader. I thought at the finish of *'Ghosts, Demons & Dolls'* that would have been the end of my short literary career, but I was wrong. The first volume was a bit of an uphill struggle for me as I really didn't know what to expect or have a clue how to go about it at the end of this one I may find it has been no different, but I just felt the need to put together another one. I again thank Twitter and Facebook too this time, for giving me so much help in finding the people who were more than willing to help in putting this one together. As previously, I shall be writing these as the stories are given, with no changes. However, I may change or omit names/places as requested.

The Paranormal field is still as fascinating for me as I hope it is for you. There are so many stories people are unwilling to tell and I hope that in this volume you may find a few of them. I have been lucky enough that some of the previous contributors are willing to go through this with me again, and I sincerely thank them all so much; without these daring, brave people you wouldn't be reading this! I STILL haven't been on a Ghost Hunt, but now I think I'm just waiting for an invitation from someone to take me (must remember to take the smelling salts!). I hope you enjoy the stories here, I found that they are all just as fascinating as the ones in the first volume! I have also been fortunate to include in this volume more interviews, which I hope you enjoy.

At this point I should also say that I have taken into account some of the comments from my last offering to you. It had been said that they would like to know what I think and it might be good for me to comment on them, but I don't consider that this is about me or what I think –

you all know by now that I am a believer; these are about you. However, I will go a step further on this, and I shall be asking the views from someone who, unlike me, is very sceptical about everything to do with the paranormal field. I would even go so far as to say that they are a total disbeliever. I shall let you make up your own mind, of course. They have been good enough to put a section on their thoughts at the back of the book. If they have said anything you disagree with, please don't be offended – after all, it is only their personal view.

I have also tried to get in more stories for you in this edition. It is still not easy to get them in! So again Reader, I invite you to sit back, pull the curtains and settle down to a good read, and don't forget: these stories may not all be scary, but they are all true; some are very short, they are also the same things that could happen in any house, maybe even yours? You may want to go and check to see what those thumps and bumps *really* are! Please enjoy.

Sceptic's comment

I feel very privileged to have been asked to add my commentary to this book. Yes, I am a sceptic; I believe in what can be seen, touched and measured. I grew up in a place where many people had "seen" ghosts. I spent many hours in those same places and have never experienced anything that could not be explained within the physical world. Having said that, I am open minded enough to have my point of view changed should evidence be presented. At the end of this book you will see my comments; these are just my thoughts and views as I read the stories. You never know, by the end of this book I may not be such a sceptic.

THE STORIES

This bewildering and scary story is from Stephanie of P. Act Paranormal. This is mainly about her son who had this happen to him, and he's only a little fella! It seems he might follow in Mum's footsteps when he gets older! I wonder why children are more open to the paranormal and why a lot of us seem to lose that ability when we become adults? It might be that we accumulate too much in our brains and it takes over the part where we were able to see and hear them so easily! That's a discussion for another day, I think.

Although I have been investigating the paranormal for over six years now, my most prominent experiences seem to happen when I am not investigating at all. It seems I am the one being haunted most of the time – after all, it was a shadow figure that found me and led me to my passion for the paranormal. This story I am about to share is my most memorable and aggressive experience so far.

It all began the day following my father's tragic passing. My mother and I were sitting in the living room in silence and my son, who was nearing the age of four, was playing with Matchbox cars on the couch. Considering his young age he was completely unaware of the situation; he didn't understand the concept of death.

I began to notice he had this frightened look on his face and appeared to be following something with his eyes. As he was doing this he was watching the ceiling. I was in the process of asking him what was wrong when he stopped me mid-sentence and said "Shhh! It will hear you!"

At this point my stomach dropped, and he went on to state that there was a Demon crawling on the ceiling! I kept looking at where he was looking, but never saw anything. This went on for a good five minutes, then his mood changed. That's when you could see the relief set in by his facial expression. He was still looking at the ceiling, but he was fixated on a place on the left of the room. He then said, "It's OK, Michael is here to 'tect us."

This struck me as odd, but then he went on to name a few details about this "Michael". He said, "He's covered in blue and has a big knife."

My mother and I both came to the same conclusion that he was speaking of the Archangel. However, we had no idea how he would have knowledge of this. Astounded, we just continued to watch him as he walked through the living room towards the fire place. At about the time he reached it, he had a huge smile on his face and gave out an excited sigh and yelled out my father's first name. To make this even more interesting, he didn't know him by his first name, he only knew him as "Papaw." We were pretty much at a loss for words. He continued to surprise us and his next topic was asking why my dad was wearing different clothes and could go through the wall? There were a few moments of silence after this, then he continued to play as before.

Things began to get weird again as we began to go to his bedroom to put him to bed. To get to his bedroom we first had to pass through the den. As we passed through the den he started to speak of this Demon again. He was trying to tell me what the Demon said, when he could do this, and began to speak in whispers and what sounded like "tongues." This was something I couldn't bear to hear. I stopped him before he could finish every time. This was something you definitely shouldn't be hearing from a child. After many failed attempts he finally stopped trying to relay this message. I was then able to get his mind off this being and take him to bed. Little did I know that this was just the start of many phenomena throughout my home.

The next morning my mother called me and told me

there was somebody trying to break in; she explained that the doorknob kept shaking and rattling. To be safe I armed myself with my pistol and walked to the door – only to find no one was there. I found it strange that my dog wasn't barking considering that she barks at everyone who comes onto our property.

Throughout the rest of the day there were many unusual occurrences, starting with the sound of crying at various times. I heard crying coming from the den area and went to comfort what I thought was my mom. To my surprise, the room was empty. I then realized my mother hadn't even gotten there yet. The same thing happened to my mom, but she thought the crying was my son or me. My son even mentioned a girl crying in the den. When my mother and I told one another about the crying experience we knew things were getting more active.

Later that night my mother, sister and I were in the bedroom talking – and that's when we heard this terrible crashing noise across the hallway in my son's room. We all three ran to see what it was, thinking someone was in there. Again we were wrong. The light was off and the room was empty. As we examined the room we found the source of the crash we had heard. My son had this small shelf in the side of his closet where there were many of his items. Every item on that shelf was spread over the floor at least six feet away! The shelf was still completely intact. We knew we were in for a ride at this point.

My two inside dogs started to act strangely about the house. The rooms they would most frequently stay in became their most avoided places. They would go towards certain areas of the house and begin to growl and back away. At one point we kept hearing this strange noise. We went to see what was making the noise and found it was coming from the bathroom. The toilet seat was actually shaking and one of the dogs was in the hallway while watching it and growling. She began to slowly back up then she yelped and jumped back over a foot in distance.

She ran away terrified. We were so lost at this point, as it was like nothing we had ever experienced.

It was that same night and my mother was lying in bed when she heard a terrible noise coming from the closet. She described it as the "sound of bones breaking". After she had finally fallen asleep, she randomly sat straight up in bed and recalled seeing a dark shadow come from beneath the bed! The shadow came up towards her and she actually felt it pass through her body. That is when the entity became even more terrifying. We then knew we had to get rid of it, and fast. Despite our experience with the paranormal, we knew we would need assistance.

We then contacted a friend and pleaded for help – we had no idea that this would be a three-week process. We began doing rituals representing our friend's culture in the removal attempts. We had to do these preparations a week before moving forward. After we were ready to attempt removing this apparition from our home, we started out with more typical removal techniques with white sage being an example. After carrying out this process daily for one week we had seen a decrease in activity, but we still had some activity present; this included objects moving, terrifying sounds and feelings. During our final week of the removal process we would have things happen while our friend was attempting his sage clearing. At one point our pictures began falling off the walls. He then came to the conclusion he was going to have to use a more powerful method, during which we were not allowed to be present due to his cultural rules. I must say that the ritual he conducted was the answer; when this was finalized we never had anything related to this entity again.

This next one is from my husband Roger, which is very strange as he pretty much is a non-believer!

He remembers his father saying that a long time before Roger was born, Roger's sister and his father were in their bedrooms in the old Farmhouse, and it was quite late at night. It was during the winter and there was a heavy snow on the ground. Everything was silent, as it is when at the farm at night, but even more so when there is snow on the ground which serves to muffle every sound.

The old Farmhouse is not there now as a new house has been built away from where the old one stood. The old Farmhouse was built almost in the yard of the farm. At the side of the yard to the left, is a bridle path (trackway) that leads to a field. The old coach road used to run up this track and then diagonally to the left towards the main road.

On this night they were just getting ready for bed when they heard a coach with four-in-hand (four horses), being driven past the front door. This was impossible as the path outside is only about four feet wide – even a modern day car has to squeeze down it.

They heard the jingling of the reins and other items of tack, also the rolling of the wheels going past at quite a fast pace. Roger's father looked out but could see nothing, as it was very dark. He went to bed and thought no more of it. He got up early each morning at about three o'clock to get ready to go and get the cows in for milking, and as he went down to the yard he could see the tracks of the carriage wheels and imprints of the horses hooves. As he turned up the track to get the cows, the imprints continued up the track then veered off to the left, just where the old coach road would have been. The strangest part of all was that there were now hedges and fences across the fields to separate the cows from the sheep, but right through them both was a carriage-sized hole in the snow-covered hedges where something had passed through them! The fences were not broken and the hedges remained unharmed. There was just a gaping hole with no snow on it! This was a very peculiar sight to greet anyone first thing in the morning and, as far as Roger knows, the phantom coach and horses has not been heard (or seen) again.

My brother Peter and I were talking a few weeks ago and he reminded me of a story that happened when I was a very young teen and he was only about nine or ten. I had forgotten it, but it stuck in his mind as he saw his first "ghost" that night and he has never forgotten it! He said I made him do it – what a lovely sister I am.

In Saltwood, where my brother Peter and I were born, there used to be a Youth Club held once a week in the Boy Scouts hut. This was near the old Church and as kids we used to tease the younger kids with ghost stories. I never knew if they were true or not, but I hoped they were!

Well – one night we were messing about and my friend Jinny and her brother told us about a so-called true ghost sighting that we were guaranteed to see if we went to the churchyard and followed certain steps. I do remember it was light and in the summertime – so no one could play any tricks on us without us seeing them. So off we went, up the road to the church.

When we got there we passed under the Lychgate (the covered gateway to the church yard) and the tomb we were looking for was off to our right. We couldn't miss it as it was the first one above ground and was built to house a whole family group and was shaped like a big stone box. There were yew trees all around the graveyard, and we stood near one of them and asked what it was we had to do? We were told we had to walk around it anti-clockwise three times and then knock on the top three times and the "ghost" would then appear. We were only kids and we were not at all sure, now that we were there, that we really wanted to do it! But – bravado won.

We all set off one behind the other, I think there were five or six of us but I can't remember who the others were. We completed our circuits and then did our knocks – then ran as fast as we could and hid behind the yew trees and watched and waited. It felt like we were there for ages waiting and we had all started to giggle and were quite relieved nothing had happened when one of the kids said

"Look! What is that?!"

Well, we all stopped laughing and sure enough, some of the kids said they could see at the far right on the top of the tomb a green/blue flame. They said it was about two feet high and shimmering. I couldn't see it at all!

Needless to say, we all ran as fast as out little legs would carry us back to the Youth Club. It was the topic of conversation for weeks and I'm sure some of the older kids went to try it, but they never said anything to us. We just went back to scrumping apples from the farmer's orchard. That was much safer!

I have again been lucky enough to be in contact with some users of Twitter and came across this newly formed paranormal group called Ghost Cr3w. Two of their members have sent me stories and this first one is from Kevin Cox who is an investigator. This team are from Lynchburg, Virginia. The Battle of Lynchburg was fought two miles outside of the town on the 17/18 June 1864. The Confederates came away with the victory. With all that history, if you can't find a ghost or two there – I don't think you'll find one anywhere!

One day when I was at home by myself (it was about eleven at night), I was in my room and nothing but darkness in the whole house, except the light on in my room. I was doing my own thing when, from the bedroom door – which was closed – I heard three knocks, right in front of me. They weren't that loud and they were not soft, but quite firm, solid knocks.

Then, not knowing what to do, I grabbed the door handle and locked it, like it was wildfire spreading through my home. I waited until my mum's boyfriend got home. I asked him if anyone had come by to the house and he said "No." I looked everywhere and couldn't find any explanation; to this day I can find no explanation. If anyone had opened the door I would have heard it as it makes a loud squeaking noise, no matter if you open it a small way or all the way, and the windows have this iron bar thingy behind them, so no one could break in. So, to this day, I have no clue what made the knocks.

This is a story from Jonathan Little, who is the founder of Ghost Cr3w, and was good enough to let me have this story which describes his first encounter with the paranormal.

When I was sixteen, my family and I had just moved into a brick-built house in the countryside that has a history of Civil War confrontation on the property. When I found out that there was bloodshed from the confrontation – involving the Confederacy and the Union – I just had to know the history behind the confrontation; what caused it and how many people lost their lives at the time.

One day my best friend asked if he could come over and stay for the night, so I invited him over to stay. As we were having a conversation, I turned my head and saw a shadow run through my closet door so, being me, I opened the closet door and saw that nothing was there. I thought, "How cool!" I just had to tell my friend about this.

When my friend arrived at my house I told him about what I had seen, just after I had finished speaking with him about coming over to stay. He just looked at me like I was making it up and didn't really take much notice of what I was telling him.

Soon after he arrived, my parents were leaving to go out and, about two hours after they had left, I noticed that I was hearing what sounded like someone wearing heavy boots walking up and down the hallway upstairs. So I turned to see if my friend was hearing what I was – and his face looked as if he had seen a ghost. I was glad to know I was not the only one hearing and seeing things!

When my parents arrived home, everyone was asleep and everything was dark. I woke up in the middle of the night and went downstairs to get a glass of milk. As I was shutting the refrigerator door, I felt I was being watched the whole time. I made my way up the stairs and I saw an old man, who looked like a soldier from the Civil War era, standing at the top of the staircase and staring at me. He had bloodshot eyes and it was difficult to see what his rank was on his arm. I was not in fear, and surprisingly I asked him who he was but he did not reply and just vanished, like vapour.

My friend was still sleeping but, all of a sudden, he came running out of my room and said that the covers had been pulled off him while he was asleep and that a mist had run through my closet door. He knew then that I had been telling the truth, and he was in a state of disbelief as to what had just happened. The next morning my friend went home and I have yet to hear from him, although it has been over four years now.

Spooky things still go on in my house, but they have made me become the ghost-hunter I am today.

Kat was kind to take time out and send these next stories to me. She is the lead investigator of the UK Shadow Seekers paranormal and they are based in the North West of England.

I have been lucky to attend lots of paranormal nights in some bizarre places; from terraced houses to amusement parks, to castles and fields that contain nothing but bricks and fountains.

A few years ago I attended a development workshop to see if I could perhaps try to become more sensitive to spirits. This was conducted over a few months, every week, in the front room of a medium I knew and respected. There we sat, in his normal-looking house on a normal street, trying to learn meditation; to be able to try to relax and open chakras and feelings I think we all lose as we grow older.

As the weeks went by, I attempted the first phase: "Put yourself in a field, look around the field. Do you see a wall? Touch the wall, the wall is safe and no one can harm you inside there. When you feel safe, sit in the middle of the field, relax, enjoy, feel the sun on you. Start to open your chakras one by one." When this meditation had an effect, I would then move on to phase two: "When you are feeling warm and safe, walk to the corner of your field. Find a gate and a gate-keeper. Eventually this will lead you down a path through a forest, and down to a river or a beach. Then, you will be able to meet your spirit guide."

At first my spirit guide was shown to me as a little girl, who would giggle at me and dance around. She would never speak, and I would never hear a sound. Eventually, this little girl turned into an old woman; "a sign of my advancement," I was advised. Again, she would never speak but would lead me and always sort of made me aware she was around. As I work shifts and long weeks, I used to practice long and hard on meditation before I fell asleep. Usually falling asleep whilst I did it! It was in doing this that caused me to have a very frightening experience, one I have never really matched since.

One night I lay on the bed and set off in my head meditating. Then, I'm assuming I fell asleep. The dream is very clear in my head even now, three years later. I found myself in a hospital ward looking at my mother who was being nursed by a much older woman (I think she was Anna, my guide). Anna left the room and, when she did, my mother was sitting up in bed and in a child's voice saying, "Get me out of here. I'm sorry. Get me out." I do not have a relationship with my mother and haven't done in over twenty years. So now, with tears in my eyes, I began shouting, "I don't want to see this!" When I woke up I was pinned to the bed – physically pinned – with such a heat across my whole body, drenched in sweat. When I looked towards the bottom of the bed, I saw for a few seconds a priest who just looked at me and, as I shut my eyes, he went.

A few weeks later, I meditated in the medium's house (I had learned my lesson at home!) when a man in a trench coat simply walked past me and tipped his hat to me. I said "hello" but got no reply and, while in the meditation state, I suddenly felt my wrists being pushed back and my neck was in pain. I also felt a pain in my chest, and then I was being pushed back into my field (my safe place). When I looked around, all I saw was a large iron cross being held towards my face. I was advised that the man in the trench coat was an astral traveller, and that some mediums can use this gift to hurt people. The pain in my chest and other places was this traveller seeking energy. I haven't meditated since.

Kat also sent me this one. It is from an investigation that Shadow Seekers UK did in Knottingley Town Hall, Yorkshire. It sounds to me like this is a very creepy place.

My very first experience without using meditation was around 2010. I had been below the building in the original foundations, which was originally a monastery (not sure on the date). We had set cameras up while the lights were on, and then moved upstairs. There was a lift in this building, so we moved upstairs in the lift to set the cameras up on the ground floor. We realized we had left the duct tape (to cover wires so no one trips over them), downstairs. I offered to go and get it. I got in the lift again and, as the doors opened downstairs, I realized that not only was I alone, it was also in total darkness. The only light came from the lift. I gulped and stepped out. I saw the tape quite close.

As I stepped out I heard a growl; it was loud and it was breathy and it wasn't a team member, and it wasn't a dog! I grabbed the tape, shut my eyes and got straight back into the lift and went upstairs quickly to tell the other members what had happened.

Later in the night, a medium picked up that a man and his dog were downstairs, and that the dog was fiercely protective of his owner who was a Benedictine monk.

This story is also from Kat, and the investigation was conducted this time at Hyde Town Hall which is in Cheshire, England. It is the place where Myra Hindley and Ian Brady were taken to be interrogated after being arrested for the Moors Murders, so named as the bodies of the five children they killed and sexually assaulted, were buried on Saddleworth Moor. The murders took place from 1963-1965. Police found four of the bodies, but one was never found. Kat writes:

I have always believed bad spirits, or demons, are simply film star creations. I think that if a person is bad in spirit, that they were also bad in life.

As members of the public, a friend and I went to Hyde Town Hall, known in history as the place the Moors Murderers (Ian Brady and Myra Hindley) were interviewed and arrested. This was also the place where the famous "mug shots" were taken of Myra Hindley.

I thought it would be funny to keep calling for Myra, asking her to show herself to us. I was, of course, warned by a medium that I should not do this and that she was a horrible spirit, however this didn't put me off. I was laughing, despite that my friend became scared at me calling for Myra to show herself, until I walked into what is now a store room, but back in the 1960's was used for interview rooms and cells. Then, BAM! I felt like someone had punched me deep in my stomach. It was such a pain I can't explain, it made me physically sick and ended my night. Once I got outside again – I was fine.

This one is the last one from Kat and took place in a private house in Bridgefield Street, Hapton, Burnley, England.

This house was mine (thankfully rented). It was over 100 years old and it was a house my partner's grandma had rented a room in 70 years before!

It all started in the kitchen, with the feeling of someone pushing past behind you. A draught would always come down the stairs, and some parts of the house were always cold. When alone in the house, you always felt worried and a bit on edge. The way the house was laid out was that you sat in the front room and you could see upstairs to the landing. While sitting there, watching TV, you would see a pair of legs coming down the stairs; look up, and the legs would be gone! This would continue so that the legs would always be seen from the corner of your eye. From time to time a door would slam upstairs, with no explanation, as there was no one up there at the time. This would continue – the more you ignored it, the more it would happen.

We went away to Poland for a weekend, and my partner's son kept an eye on the house for us. The day before we were due to come back, as he locked up the property he glanced up the stairs and saw a pair of legs, with boots on its feet, walk across the landing and into his room then slam the door. He vowed never to return, and we never did either; we moved!

Weeks passed and word had got back us that the new tenant had mentioned that her little son was talking to someone (like kids do), and we went cold. My partner mentioned the reasons as to why we had move to her grandma's. Her grandma told us that, while she had lived there, there was a man who worked in the local coal mine who had had an accident and, in her grandma's words, "When they went to identify him, there was nothing left but his legs!" I am glad we left!

These next three shorties are from Brendan Vesey. He saw my request on Twitter again and thought I might like them. He is the founder of Nocturnal Visions Paranormal and is also a tour guide for Nashville Ghost Tours.

My journey into the paranormal began in the 1980s. I lived in Marion IA (Iowa) with my family. It was another run-of-the mill day. My father and brothers were out and I was in my room playing, when suddenly I heard my mom scream for help. It was out of nowhere and I froze. I heard it again and I walked to my bedroom door. My sister came out of her room and she had heard the same thing. We went looking for mom and we searched the entire house, then we went down into the basement. We found her in the laundry room folding clothes. We asked her if she was OK? She said, "Yes" and then we asked her if she had screamed for help. She said "Nope," my sister and I looked at each other dumbfounded. We never found out where that one came from.

Another story from when I was little. I was in bed and got up for no real reason. I walked to the living room and saw a huge shadow walk in front of the window. I freaked out and went running back to bed. It could not have been the trees outside as the curtains were closed, and I am not sure what could have projected the shadow, but it helped to open my mind to other things.

The last one I have to tell you is also about this house, and it happened to my father. Again this was back in the 80s. My father came home from work one day and no one was home. He walked into his bedroom and there he saw his father. His father smiled at him and disappeared; it was as if he was checking on him one last time. His father had died in a tragic accident in the mid-70s when he fell from a fire escape that wasn't properly secured to a wall.

These stories are also from Twitter users. This is a story from a very nice lady called Anke Carver who is from Bruchal, Baden Wurttenberg, Germany. She is a former paranormal investigator and tells us this story because it is what made her become a Paranormal Investigator, as it touched her very much.

It happened a little bit more than a year after my grandfather died on August 21st 1986. I was seven years old and never believed in ghosts, demons or hauntings. Until this night came.

I woke up in the middle of the night because I heard a man calling my name. It wasn't my dad; this voice sounded strange, as though I heard it in my head. I got off the bed and walked into the dark hallway, went to the right around the corner, and there he was – standing in the middle of the doorway to the living room; my grandfather. I still remember seeing him clearly and my mum, who came out of her bedroom, had seen him too. He just stood there and looked at us, until he finally said, "Here I am." He disappeared in a second and we went back to bed, completely screwed up about what we had experienced.

My sister told me the other day that she had seen him standing in the garden. He was wearing his jeans, shirt and favourite hat. After this encounter it stopped for a little while, but this was just the beginning.

My grandmother used to go on vacation to my aunt's house, so the apartment was empty. We had had a house built for two families. We lived on the first floor and my grandparents on the second floor. We were watching TV one day and we heard moaning upstairs, footsteps we also heard, and the wooden bars in the roof sounded like they were cracking and moving. But we were wrong, because the location the sounds came from changed. We heard walking from the upper bedroom to the kitchen, then into the living room then … nothing.

One day I decided to go up there when we heard the footsteps start again. As I walked upstairs I felt a little breeze come down the stairs past me, and it carried the smell of my grandfather's aftershave with it. I was so terrified and sad at this moment, that I went back down and cried the whole day long. The noises happened almost every day and we got used to the footsteps and realized we were not imagining them.

When I was sixteen, my grandmother moved out to a retirement home because she couldn't walk anymore, and I moved into the apartment because I need some privacy. My mum came up one evening because she had had an argument with my dad, and wanted to spend the night on my couch. We both slept on the couch and woke up in the night because we heard the door open and someone walk in. We couldn't see anything or anybody, but we heard walking and a very sad sighing. The sounds moved away. The door closed and the hatch to the attic fell down.

We finally sold the house to give my grandfather the peace he needed, because we felt he is trapped inside because our love kept him with us.

Anke says "This story just made me cry because I miss him. It has been twenty-nine years and I always feel this pain in my heart."

This story is from Tony Parkes who was good enough to take the time and send me a story for this book and also sent another experience he had which is told in the first book. He is from South Devon in England. Please enjoy.

It is not really surprising that someone interested in the paranormal should live across the road from a graveyard. I don't go investigating spirits there though; I just love to walk around, photograph the flowers growing wild and read the occasional headstone and, if very lucky, see wild rabbits.

On this occasion I had a week's leave and my wife was away visiting her family. I ambled across the road for a walk around the graveyard with my camera phone, looking for potential pictures. Some of the undergrowth and foliage had been cleared from one section and I spotted an ornate headstone I hadn't noticed before. I wandered over and found, indeed, a wonderful headstone engraved with the name of two sisters that had died a few months apart. Strangely they had different family names and, even more strangely, the grave was roughly pointing south.

I took some pictures and, as I had so many questions, attempted an EVP session with the App on my phone. Sadly, a warm breeze that was blowing was loud enough, when recorded, to sound like an aircraft taking off!

As I walked home, still hoping at that point to have something recorded, I wondered if one of the sisters (or maybe both) were married. I was also wondering why they had died so soon and quite young. I decided to do some research, and found an epidemics timeline from the UK. Indeed, they had both died during the time of one of the epidemics.

I then found that, due to space limitations, graves are not always dug facing the east and that in these cases, bodies are laid on their side to face the east. I somehow felt that this was disrespectful, and the grave had plenty of space to face east. I decided to try to find out more, which

I did, but was not able to discover anything.

That night I fell asleep on the sofa with the light still on. I awoke when I felt a movement in the room. I searched around but found nothing to suggest what had woken me up. Nothing, that is, except that I felt I wasn't alone. I felt as if two people were standing just inside the room. This feeling went on for three days. I knew the house didn't usually have spirits and, when it had happened before, it had been following an investigation. Then the proverbial penny dropped! I had been attracted to the grave (called, possibly), and had attempted an EVP session. I got out my digital recorders, switched them on and said, "OK, I didn't invite you here, so it's time for you to answer some questions." Immediately the atmosphere cleared and I knew they had left. I wasn't surprised that I had captured no EVP's, and they haven't returned.

I have re-visited the grave, but don't feel the energy I felt when I first discovered the grave. I hope I didn't offend them and, in my defence, three days and nights of my unexpected visitors had taken their toll on my energy.

I am a firm believer that spirits will only follow you home if invited; that invitation includes showing a positive interest in them, inviting them to use your energy or do something to you. I still have regular visits to the graveyard, but now, like on investigations, I state the rules. No following or attachment, no harming of myself or anyone with me, and no throwing of objects.

Culz Paranormal sent me another story for this book. I am sure it won't be the last we hear from this prolific team, as previously every member sent a story. All I can say is, Viva Las Vegas! Thanks again to Keegan for this one.

Las Vegas is the gambling mecca of America and not many would think of it as a paranormal hotspot, but hey – what happens in Vegas stays in Vegas, so it makes sense.

Behind the sounds of slot machines, slurred curses and the aroma of a cigar or two, there is another realm: those visitors who found the allure of Vegas a bit too appealing to ever quite leave. Sometimes you may not even realize the person you are right next to is a ghost until after the fact.

I remember the first trip I made to Las Vegas: it was back in October 2008, not quite the age to drink or gamble, but I was there to see the shows and the architecture. If I hadn't gone into ghost hunting I would have gone in to the architectural field. So here Colin, Mark and I were doing some short videos about the history of the different casinos.

We started on the ground level but, as one can imagine, it was quite noisy for a video so we moved higher. We went up to the 22nd floor section of the hotel. Up there we could film without much disturbance.

We started filming but couldn't really get the shot of the neighbouring hotel/casino that we wanted, as we had a portion of the current hotel cutting the view in half, so we decided to go up to the very top level, which was level 25.

As we walked towards the elevator, we passed a gentleman walking towards one of the rooms at the end of the hallway (the casino was a Y-shape, rooms lining the hallway, with a single window at the end and all elevators in the middle). The gentleman was wearing a white tee shirt, blue jeans and black boots, black sunglasses and slicked-back black hair. We got to the elevator and went up the three floors, and as we walked to the window at the end, we saw a guy walk past us, going towards the elevators. White tee shirt, blue jeans, black boots, black sunglasses and slicked-back black hair! We passed him, made it to the end and there was the shot of the hotel we wanted, so filmed it and went back to our room.

There, we looked over all the footage; being documentary film-makers we film every second, even if we know we won't use it. This time –WOW – I'm glad we did. As we watched, we saw us pass the guy on the 22nd floor, as he headed to the dead end, only for us to pass the VERY SAME guy, coming from the dead end on the 25th floor!

It is a crazy realization that we passed a spirit trapped in time in this hotel, and didn't even know it. Like I said, what happens in Vegas stays in Vegas, and clearly this guy had an attachment to the City or, at least, the hotel. It is some of the craziest footage, not for being spooky or out of this world, but because the spirit looked as real as you or me. So, next time you are in Vegas talking to someone, just remember that they may not still be here!

Keegan from Culz also sent me in this story from Mark Culz. Another creepy one for you to enjoy!

In Volume 1 of *Ghosts, Demons & Dolls*, I told the story of the ghost truck in Aurora, Colorado. Well, this time around I've got another story from about the same time, about the same location.

A little story about the site: there is an urban legend about hearing Native American drums playing at night, but let's get this out there first – it's all been debunked. Listening to the "drums," we figured out it's only the sounds of the oil rigs near the site. But, while the "drums" seem to be a myth, the location has been known to have quite a few deaths, usually due to poor driving on the one-car-width road at night.

We have also caught some decent evidence there and,

barring the episode where a bad spirit was so overwhelming that Keegan began to puke, the site is known mainly for one very nice spirit of a girl who died in a car crash. OK – onto the story!

We were below the bridge on site, doing some EVP work. It was a calm night and the grass was not moving, so there was no wind and the sky was clear. Only the moonlight cut through the darkness. We asked questions, did readings to test for electrical spikes, and watched to be careful not to fall into the stream. Nothing was happening. It is actually quite common on investigations. The spirit world doesn't work on command.

Keegan, Scott, Colin and I sat around the recorder waiting for something to happen, that's when I glanced towards Scott's truck. Standing next to it was a tall, dark shadow-like figure, about as tall as the truck, but the figure was no body builder!

Of course, we thought somebody was trying to break into Scott's truck, , which was a good 100 feet from us, so we rushed towards it and in the flat Iowa landscape the intruder had no-where to hide, but he didn't run – he simply just vanished into thin air.

The only calling card it left was the fingerprints and lines drawn on the windows.

Mark Culz also sent me this story from a few years ago. It is actually the prequel to the one the guys sent me for my previous book. If you read it – well, that's for you to decide. All I will say is that this team really goes above and beyond what I expected of them when we first contacted each other! You can check out the Lawrence EVP on their YouTube channel.

We were back at Memmen Ridge, Castle Rock in Colorado. If you read Erica's first book *Ghosts, Demons & Dolls*, you will know that Keegan's first story also took place here, but this story predates that one by almost three years.

See, we were back there investigating Lawrence (our favourite and most popular EVP on YouTube) to date. We had just collected some new evidence during our research into who had owned the land in the previous decades, and thought we may finally be able to solve the mystery of Lawrence.

The night was clear; a few clouds, but up on the hill there is a dense forest, so the branches create a thick cover over the forest floor, almost like one giant umbrella and even if it was raining it wouldn't affect us too much. But, like I said, the night was clear and we had just passed the point on the trail where the video had captured the apparition, at the same time the EVP caught the voice Lawrence.

Up to this point the investigation was silent – after only a few hours this is really quite common – so we decided to head further into the forest. Nearly fifty feet up, the dirt path went to the right and the left side opened up and revealed the "hanging tree." Some locals have said that this tree saw its share of hangings back in the Old West!

We did a Spirit Box session here: Keegan placed it near the tree and asked the questions, Colin took photographs and I (Mark), filmed. During the session we heard some responses, we couldn't tell what they said unfortunately as they spoke in Spanish and the reacting voices didn't last long, so we packed up and headed up the hill towards the trail.

We followed the trail and did some investigating in the clearing overlooking the City and headed back.

Overall, the investigation seemed to be a lost cause. That's when it happened! As we neared the "hanging tree" we heard rustling in the trees and brush. When we got close enough I spotted it! It looked like a large, very odd shaped cat shadow, but the shadow wasn't *on* anything, it was just there! It wasn't like a shadow person experience; the cat apparition was just there like you or me; except it had no features!

I grabbed the camera and sprinted towards it. It hopped a little then morphed into the tree – just like that; vanishing into thin air! It was such a short experience, but the fact we saw this cat-like shadow stays with me every time we have gone back. It was watching us then – maybe it watches everyone? Could it be the cause of the hair standing up on the backs of necks of people? Sometimes I think so. Maybe it is a lost spirit that had once been hung there? We don't really know as we never saw it again.

Well – now that I think of it, did Keegan, Josh and Sam experience the shadow cat? In his story, in the previous book, whatever spirit had followed them did it the same way a cat hunts. Maybe it was the shadow cat keeping an eye on us all these years later? Just food for thought!

Here is a story from Aaron Buchold, he is the Case Manager with the Culz Team.

My interest in the paranormal goes back to my childhood. Out of all the evidence I have captured, or that of my fellow investigators, the most frightening and face-to-face encounter I had ever, goes back to that time.

I was about nine or ten years old, and I had a friend stay at my house overnight. We were running around the house with toy guns playing GI Joe. I lived in a house with a basement, a family room which was the TV room, kitchen/living room and upstairs guest room to the left, my brother's room at the end and my parent's room was first on the right. The second room on the right was a connecting bathroom. My friend and I were chasing each other around with the toy guns, hiding behind couches and corners of the house.

I ran upstairs to hide from him in my parent's room, with my back to the door, and he was behind me in their bathroom, ducking down on the floor. Leaning against the door, I looked to my right and saw a shadow staring out of the window. The shadow was the same height as me, standing still, just gazing outside. Keep in mind the whole upstairs didn't have a single light on. The only light came through the window. I looked at this shadow, very confused, thinking my friend was standing there.

I called his name and there was no response; he was still hidden in the bathroom! I called out one more time and the shadow turned around – at that same time I heard my friend respond from the bathroom. When I realized that was him, I dropped my toy gun and ran downstairs to my mother in total fear. When I ran downstairs, seconds later so did my friend. We used to keep a dirty clothes hamper in the hallway, he said it had opened wide then slammed shut! Since then I have never forgotten that moment, and have told this story exactly as it happened. My mum remembers that night exactly as well. I never understood why I was chosen to witness him or her, but that is something I will never forget. Since then I have always known, and found evidence, that we are not alone when we pass away. We still have a voice; it just takes an ear to hear us.

Aaron from Culz has given this story, it just goes to show that loved ones still think about us even when they've left this world and moved on to the next. They have also said that they are so glad that I am doing another book as they have so many stories to tell, and it's been so much fun remembering them all. They can't wait for this one!

My wife, Andrea, lost her father to Parkinson's disease and, on top of that, brain cancer. After being diagnosed, with only a little time left, he had continued to strive, beyond their expectations. Finally slowing down with time, he decided to go to sleep. We saw it on Skype, so he didn't really get one-on-one time with his daughter, and he loved her very much!

We travelled to Florida for the funeral. On that trip we gathered some of his belongings for personal memories. I unfortunately only knew him for three years of his time here, he was a great person. He was funny and always carried a light in his heart.

One of our fondest memories was when he came out of his room; he always pushed a button on a "fart" machine and groaned "Aaaah!" So, Andrea and I decided to take this machine home.

One night, back home in Colorado, we were sitting back watching TV in the living room. The "fart" machine was on the kitchen counter over by us. All of a sudden the machine went off! We looked at each other, knowing that he had made his presence known! I grabbed the digital recorder and we started talking to him. We both knew he was there, you could *feel* his presence.

I asked him to knock on the wall and we heard a couple of thumps, but we quickly de-bunked it as the neighbour in the apartment next door. Then I asked him to give me three knocks or to press the button on the "fart" machine because it made Andrea laugh.

We got a voice on the recorder. It said "Andrea – I love you." When I heard that EVP I felt he was there to make sure she was OK, and to let her know he was OK and to say goodbye, he sounded very at peace. Not everybody gets that chance to say goodbye, but he made sure she got that.

Later, Andrea's mum came to visit. We played her the EVP and she looked at us with sad eyes and said, "That was him. It was Ted's voice." We also captured orbs around our apartment, but the EVP will always let us know he's in a good place and his light still shines.

R.I.P. TED SCHWARTZ March 3rd 1946 – April 26th 2012

As you know, Culz have been very prolific contributors of stories for the last book and also this one too! They have no idea how much I appreciate it! I just wish I lived closer, then I could go hunting with them perhaps? This story is set out a little differently, more like a conversation between them and you, the reader. I like this as it feels more "chatty."

Keegan Cool: My first story, that I told Erica for her first book, *'Ghosts, Demons and Dolls'* (2015), took place at Memmen Ridge in Castle Rock, and at the end I briefly mentioned how we had done an investigation there around a Ouija board that totalled a car. Well, here is the story.

Alan Hickson: We were helping a mom who had contacted the group after her kids, as well as some others, had been using a Ouija board. Something had followed them home and it had gotten to the point of pushing one of the kids near suicide. Another had run away from home; the kid of a preacher.

Keegan Cool: Originally we had met the mother, who wishes to remain unnamed, at a park near the Ridge. She at first wanted to know how knowledgeable we were in the paranormal field, as she had some knowledge, and wanted to make sure the group was legit before she entrusted the group in trying to bring some peace to her family. Joining us during this story will be Josh Williams, our friend from the YouTube channel Sound in Reverse, who was also on the investigation.

Josh Williams: The kids had been doing the Ouija board sessions with little to no activity, 'til one night when, according to the kids, something seemed to have attached itself to the group, and some of the kids began freaking out.

Keegan Cool: Like Alan said before, the kids started going

off the deep end after these sessions, leading to one running away, one going suicidal and one apparently being attracted to the board. She drove to the location without (as she said), "Having any control over herself." Out of fear of the spirit continuing its hold over everyone, a few of them went back to the Ridge, tore the board apart, and buried it. They also told their mother and that's when she contacted us. She wanted to see if we could help, and we agreed to take on the challenge, but first we had to find the board.

Alan Hickson: We had met with the kid's mom at the Memmen Ridge open space parking lot, and she began to help fill in the gaps on the situation with me and the rest of the Culz Paranormal team, who hadn't met with her during that first meeting. The mother had brought one of her kids (not the ones originally involved in the sessions) and together we looked all over the open space. Heck, we must have covered five acres of space trying to find the board! Finally, after what felt like hours of searching, we found it at the base of a tree near the main path.

Keegan Cool: For a while there I didn't think we would find it; no one searching for it had been there when it was buried. It was like looking for a needle in a haystack. The mother finally contacted the son who buried it, and he told us exactly where it was, and we made our way to the tree.

Josh Williams: We dug out the board, which lay not even half a foot in the dirt, and began reassembling it, because it was torn apart as they figured that would stop it. I put the pieces together and we began our investigation. What do I remember about it once the board was together? Hurt my hands even touching it, and there was a strange wind around the area. I had headphones on listening to the EVP in real time, and I could hear deep breathing the entire time.

Keegan Cool: The air felt heavy, like you needed a knife to cut it; it was weird, very weird.

Alan Hickson: After digging in the dirt, one of our former team members went and blessed some water away from us, in the hope of using it in the process of trying to shut down whatever evil had followed the kids home. We were also hoping it wouldn't harm anyone else, and maybe we could close the portal. I got the strange feeling that we were all being watched. I could feel the hair on my neck stand up; it felt like someone had a hair dryer pointed at the back of my head.

Josh Williams: We all said a prayer and put the water on the board, that's when we started wandering off.

Alan Hickson: The hot, heavy breathing had left my immediate location and I had begun to hear crashing of oak branches. I thought it could have been a deer, being mildly sceptical of the situation at the time. What must have been a half hour later (that felt like double) I noticed a light in the trees just down the hill from our location, then another and another. My brother Adam and I began to follow these lights. I got nervous, being aware of my surroundings, heading down into a valley-like area covered in pine trees; it had looked almost like white Christmas tree lights, they seemed like they were all over. Dead ahead was a bright red orb, about the size of a ping pong ball. Just after I had noticed it, I felt trapped – like I was about to be ambushed – and the hot breathing was back on the back of my skull. Now though, I had an overwhelming feeling of anger. As to what I was mad at, I have no idea!

Keegan Cool: A former member had taken off in a different direction than Alan, and so a couple of us followed him. It was the classical set-up. The "herd" was being thinned out, the spirit was separating us; predators do this to find the weakest members. Demons have also been known to do this.

Alan Hickson: I noticed the lights all disappeared. I don't have any idea how long I had been standing there, but after this we re-joined the rest of the team.

Josh Williams: Everyone came back together unharmed, and we were about to head out when the son got a call saying one of the girls planned to come find the board that night. We couldn't just leave the board there for more people to mess with; for all we knew the spirit was attached to it. Keegan spoke up and took the board with him, putting it in a shoe box in his trunk.

Keegan Cool: I figured it was the only way to keep the kids from any more harm: take the board away. I had an empty shoe box, so we put it in that and put it in the trunk of my car. I figured it was all over, but it had only begun. Up to that point my Lancer had run fine, with no problems whatsoever. I always kept it maintained and changed the oil regularly. But after only three years of owning the car, and a couple of days of having the board, things began to break, left, right and centre! Transmission began failing, the computer system would malfunction, a tire deflated, the struts broke, oil leaks, the CD player would switch to songs by itself, or turn itself to another channel. It's worth a mention I also always felt like something was there in the car with me, in the back passenger seat. I could always feel it looking at me in the rear view mirror. But, at this point, I never thought it could be related to the problems. But things kept breaking faster than they could be fixed, and at one point the car struggled to move, so it was time to get a new car. I bought a WRX with barely any miles on it and traded in the Lancer. Before I could head home, I had to empty my stuff from one car to another, and I put the Ouija board in the new car, still not connecting anything (even though I refused to take it in my house). I drove the car home and, on the second drive ever, on my way to work, it broke down. Completely burned out! I had to have it towed and that's when it hit me: the damn Ouija board. Up to the point it entered the Lancer, no problems; after, though, the car died – now a second car … very strange things indeed.

Needless to say, I quickly removed that board from my car, and to this day not a single problem with it. The car feels empty, unless there are other people in it. As at the time of this story being written for Erica's second book, we still have the Ouija board, but we have a plan to hide it away from people forever. The board is haunted.

Alan Hickson: That board and the place would be forever haunting to the kids who had played with an alternative fire. Some would continue to regret it long after our trip to the place that had once been a place of relief and fun with friends. It had turned dark. I can only hope they learned a lesson on the gates of evil, and what can happen when you poke at it. This was an experience I would not soon forget, as being a hunter who is tactically aware I had allowed myself to be ambushed by something that made my very blood boil.

Keegan Cool: Before this I had never had an experience with an Ouija board and, let's be honest, the board itself isn't old and mystic. It is credited as being invented in 1890, and no evidence has been shown to say it works. But what happens when you're somewhere you may think is harmless, but has paranormal activity like Memmen Ridge has? You're telling anything that it's ok to talk to you. Harmless spirits won't harm you, but when you're giving things you can't see permission to talk and mess with you – well, it can end badly. It's not the board – heck! You can probably use a blanket, piece of fruit, old shoe – it's the giving permission to unseen forces that it's OK.

I can't stop you from using Ouija boards, but I can say: be careful, the paranormal world can be dangerous, and we do get cases where people have bitten off more than they can chew.

Here is another great story from the Culz guys, please enjoy!

Keegan Cool: Most of the group may be from Colorado, and at this point we all live there, but there is another state that calls to us. The state of Kentucky, which joined the Union as the 15th state on June 1st 1792 has a very rich history or, should I say, Paranormal History.

It's known for its big stories and big locations, the many oddities and legends, be it Waverly Hills in Louisville Kentucky, or Bobby Mackey's Music World in Wilder. There is the legend of The Goat Man or even the dozens of Bigfoot or UFO's sightings over the years.

I know the first time I went out, I was really excited to learn more about the state's long-running paranormal history.

I arrived in Kentucky at the Louisville Airport with my uncle Mark on February 6th 2011. My dad picked us up and we went back to his house. He told us about a recent ghost experience he had, where an apparition ran in front of his car only to disappear in the middle of the road. He also talked about a deer charging the car. Both stories were backed up by other locals, as well as the book *Weird Kentucky*, which talks about the disappearing ghost and the "demon" deer that charges cars. That was all the experiences we had that night, as we finished off the night watching the Green Bay Packers defeat the Pittsburgh Steelers in Super Bowl 45.

The next morning, my dad, Ron, took us to the bridge where the Goat Man is supposedly seen. The bridge is old and a very cool relic left in time but, at the same time, do not get on the bridge! It is still active and people have been killed on it so please – don't go on it.

So, overall, the three days there were fun but very quiet on the paranormal front. Any good paranormal investigator will tell you the paranormal realm isn't always active.

At the airport I found the book *Weird Kentucky*, and

dived into its legends. I returned to Kentucky not long after, once again with my uncle Mark, as well as my Yia ya (Greek for Grandmother, yes I'm part Greek) but this time we also came with some equipment. Mark had brought his night vision camera, while I brought the EVP recorder. The nights we spent investigating, and in one picture, we got a face looking back at us; but that's not what this trip will be remembered for, no – something else was at work here.

Mark Cool: So, we were investigating around Ronnie's place, mom was asleep on the couch so Keegan and I were trying to be quiet and decided to head to the back yard. We arrived outside on a cool summer's night, the moon was full and the trees were still. We weren't experiencing too much, but we were hearing noises; something tumbling in the long grass, something moving through the trees. It was loud and rough and it had Keegan and me on edge – what could it be? A deer maybe? There was nothing else too large out there, maybe a stray horse or cow? It continued and stopped; and then the trees blew in the wind, in the wind the tree down the hill to the right of the house looked like a skull laughing. Very creepy indeed, but still probably just us imagining it. We went inside with only the sounds of something moving in the brush on the recorder.

The next night I heard Keegan yelling, "Get over here!" I grabbed the camera and ran over. What I saw was a strange animal-like shape near the barbed wire fence. It wasn't a deer or cow or bear or anything like I've seen. It just stayed there, not moving; it looked like it was on all fours and swaying a bit. We watched for a while before it too disappeared. Maybe it was a Bigfoot?

Keegan Cool: Now, I am not going to say it was Bigfoot; I have no proof of some hairy ape-like creature running around the Americas, and if you watch Culz Fun Facts, my friend Josh and I talk about how the legendary Yeti is most likely just a bear. And don't get me started on the whole inter-dimensional Bigfoot theory. But this was a weird animal, possibly just a ghost or spirit animal. We already have caught animal ghosts on audio before, we have uploaded a Ghost Dog barking on to our YouTube channel, but who knows what it was for sure? All I know was it was black in colour and at least as high as the fence, though it did seem to be crouching. Very well, it could have been a spirit of some long extinct animal, a demon or hahaha – the Goat Man! Haha – no way!

Mark Cool: On a trip I went out to Ronnie's, just with dad this time. I heard a loud screech-like sound, it made it a few times. It was very strange and very unique. I haven't heard anything like it before.

Keegan Cool: I ended up going back to Louisville in the fall, for orientation for school at the University of Louisville. After the three days spent there, my dad took my brother, Colin, and sister, Mariah, to Waverly Hills Sanatorium just outside Louisville. Man, what a place! The drive up to it is a long road surrounded by trees, and then it opens up revealing the Goliath of a building known as Waverly Hills Sanatorium. It is a very well-known location, as it has been featured on shows like 'Ghost Adventures' and 'Ghost Hunters'. It opened up in 1910 to help patients who had contracted the "white plague" or tuberculosis. It added extensions in 1912 and 1914 and, due to the outbreak, the new five-story building was built in 1926. The cases reduced after the medicine introduced to fight it, and the Sanatorium closed in 1961. It reopened as a nursing home Woodhaven Geriatric Centre in 1962. It closed again in 1982 due to rumoured patient neglect. It was been estimated that over 8,000 breathed their last breaths in Waverly Hills.

We were able to do a short tour/investigation, where we were lead through all the haunted rooms Waverly could offer. At one point we were allowed to walk down a hallway. My brother – Colin – went first and, half way down the hallway, the shadows consumed him. It was 2 o'clock though, in the middle of the day and the sunlight was still going strong. The chills got us from time to time, and we even saw a shadow-like apparition darting down the hall.

Colin Cool: I remember walking down and, when I got half way they said 'stop!' I stood there and I could see them fine but, from what they said, the shadows slowly crept out of the doorways and ceiling and completely engulfed me. I know while I was down there in a doorway, I saw a shadow – maybe two or three feet tall – peeking out at me. As I stared at it, it darted quickly down the hallway; I could see it as it passed the doorways.

Keegan Cool: We also saw a rose left for one of the patients who had disappeared. It's such a cool place and it shouldn't be long before we do a full scale investigation there!

As soon as we got back to my dad's, I listened to the EVP recorder and, sure enough, we had caught some. The first one was faint and said, "YUP;" the second was a bit clearer but dragged out it said, "I take Last Stand." It sounded like an older gentleman, possibly on his deathbed. But the clearest is the most chilling. You can hear talking and then you hear a girl say, "Daddy," as clear as day. It's always sad when you hear a child's voice, even more so now that I am a father. A child looking for their parents is even more heart-breaking.

If you want to hear these, you can find them on our YouTube page; the "Daddy" one is the one of the most chilling EVPs I've ever heard, and I've heard them say my name, so that's saying something!

Overall, Kentucky is such a wonderful place for the

Paranormal. These are just a few of our stories but, honestly, if you wanna go find the paranormal, go to Kentucky – it's waiting for you!

Andrea Halford is the founder of Paranormal Searchers in Kent, England. She contributed to the last book and has also been kind enough to take the time to submit these two stories. I know I couldn't live in this house, but you can get used to anything I suppose! I should also say: the house in Lewis Road she refers to is a story you can find in Volume 1 of 'Ghosts, Demons and Dolls'.'

The year is 2004 and the month is February. It is the 18th, which I remember as it was my oldest daughter's eighteenth birthday, and she was away for the move into the house in Chaucer Way in Dartford. The house was a 3-bedroomed semi-detached. The house was built on a Roman burial ground, but that was so long ago we were not bothered.

This story is true and still ongoing, so not everything will be in chronological order as we have been here eleven years now. I will do my best to keep events as orderly as possible, but that will be hard as things happen almost daily now, even if it is small stuff!

We moved in on a Friday, my eldest daughter and her boyfriend were away; my son and younger daughter were with their grandparents. Friday night was our first night in our new home. We hadn't had anything nasty happen since 1997 at the Lewis Road house and this house was quite a new building, only four years old. There would be six of us living here: myself, my husband Tony, Jake my son, two daughters and the eldest daughter's boyfriend.

Friday was spent unpacking and then settling in for the night. Saturday was more unpacking for me while Tony brought decorating materials and started to decorate each room from top to bottom. I helped most of the time and, on Sunday, my eldest daughter and her boyfriend arrived home and joined in the work. It wasn't too long before we had all the bedrooms decorated and new flooring laid. On Monday a friend came over and helped fit new furniture together.

Monday night it all started! It had taken just three days before the house showed us it had the potential to be a bit weird.

The whole family and a friend were in the lounge, all the bedrooms had been finished and our son Jake and his sister had returned. We had been busy unpacking and so had fish and chips in the lounge. That is when the first thing occurred.

We were sitting there eating and chatting, when all of a sudden we heard what sounded like a stick being dragged across the railings on the stairs. The kind of clack-clack noise, as if a child had run a stick across the wooden rods holding up the hand rail that went upstairs. It was loud and went on quite a long time. We sat in silence, all open-mouthed as we were all together and there was no one else in the house. I got up and went into the hall, which was just off the lounge, but there was no one about, which we knew there wouldn't be. I looked for a reasonable explanation but found none. I recreated the sound with my finger running across the slats – everyone shouted, "That's it!" I returned to the lounge and didn't discuss it further as there was nothing to say, just "that was weird!"

Then, almost immediately, we heard a cat cry; it was so loud a few of us stopped eating and went in search. Our three cats had not arrived yet. We all agreed the noise had come from the bottom cloakroom, which was right next to the lounge and in the same hallway as the previous noise. Again there was nothing. Again we said nothing except – we all agreed – it had been a cat.

So, we are now into week one. Everywhere is decorated from top to bottom in ten days. My eldest daughter and her boyfriend have the smallest double bedroom. This next bit I must explain so you will know why my daughter was thinking as she did. The house we moved into was in a block of three. Ours was at the end and next to a fence with woodland behind it. Our property was the second largest in the road, with a big back garden and a huge piece of land at the side. We had one neighbour, and at the front of the house was our drive and a big, open off-road parking area. Our fence ran along our drive and then carried along the side of our house and along the garden. (This fence and woodland will become important later on). The house in the middle was small and, sad to say, my eldest daughter and her boyfriend had been friends with the boy who had lived there. I say 'had lived' as he died when he was sixteen from a drugs overdose.

My eldest daughter and boyfriend started telling us that their TV was turning itself on when they were asleep. Of course, with Lewis Road under our belts, we knew this could happen but at first we suspected the electrics. We had them checked but found nothing wrong with them. But it kept happening. They then said that the boy from next door was visiting them. They said he was turning the TV on and had now started to move things around too. We never witnessed this, but much later on in the story this room does prove to be strange, and that is putting it mildly!

They insisted this was happening every night, so I said to unplug it, which they did. The next night they were frantic; they had been woken by a voice calling their names. My reaction was: maybe they had heard something else. That was until they insisted things in the room were also moving. They were waking up to find things on the bed. They had found books, jewellery and things like that. I couldn't disbelieve them now, not after we had all heard the sound the railings made, the cat crying. Now there was the trouble with the electrics and things being moved and a voice.

We had to accept that perhaps there was something/someone else in the house. It didn't feel vicious or dangerous; nothing like Lewis Road had. But I had to admit I was getting a little suspicious that perhaps it was going to happen again. The children didn't know about all that had gone there, so they had nothing to go on.

Between 1997 and 2004 we had lived in two other places and nothing strange had happened in either of them. I had continued to study mediumship, but had stepped it up to cover college courses, the mechanics etc. as I needed knowledge after what we went through.

The next few months went by, with my daughter and boyfriend still insisting the boy from next door was haunting them. We all began to hear little knocks, bangs and weird unexplained noises, but we couldn't find them, or really didn't take any notice. We just lived with it. Every time we got used to something happening, something new would start. It had started with the bannister, the cat and the electrics. Then there were the things being taken and moved and now – there was something on the bed at night. It was almost as if it was stepping up its game.

Around six months into 2004, the TVs in our room kept blowing up somehow. We would turn them on and watch them for about ten minutes – then, puff, they were gone. This started to happen a lot.

We would use a spare set, buy a new one and it would last months before it too blew up. So, now we were getting stuff going on too. In my daughter's room she was still having issues with the TV, lights and things moving. However, things in there had escalated, and they claimed something was jumping on the bed and walking on them.

We continued like this for the rest of 2004 into 2005. By now we had been through three new TVs in eighteen months. The noises were happening more often too. We began to hear footsteps on the stairs when there was no one there. All these oddities were unexplainable. But not once did I disbelieve my daughter. They got used to it and life continued in this way for another year.

In 2006, my daughter and boyfriend moved into their own place. So my youngest daughter moved into the room they had shared. She had previously been sharing a split room with my son, who was now ten. As she was now fifteen, her sister moving out was welcomed.

2006 – It stepped up its game again.

By September 2006 my son started secondary school and his sister further education and doing A-levels.

So we go into 2007. My daughter started sleep walking. She never did this as a youngster. She had also started waking up screaming; this is also something she had never done. She is now sixteen years old and acting really oddly. Then she starts saying that there is something in her room that wakes her. Her TV is turning on and off and things are being moved. All the same things her sister reported, but she blames her younger brother and wants a lock on her room. We do this, but things still disappear.

By this time, I have now joined my first paranormal team and I am their medium. So I increase my learning into Demonology, Healing, Cryptids and Ufology. The team I am with don't seem to be very knowledgeable or equipped for public questions, so look to me for answers. I am happy to learn more, especially with what is going on at home.

Now we are 2008 and have lived here for four years, and have both daughters reporting the same things happening in that bedroom. Things disappear, something jumps on the bed and electrical items have a life of their own.

These things are going on in our bedroom too, now. The only bedroom not affected is my son's. So we continue to live with the weirdness and just talk to it, as if it's a real person. We ask nicely to 'please be quiet tonight,' or, if the TVs start, we would ask, 'please don't break them, or not tonight.'

Then things take a different turn. We discovered the woodland next to our house had been a smallpox cemetery, but it was supposed to end at my garden fence. We found a grave, still intact, ten feet from our fence. We thought 'OK, at least we are not built on it ...'

Spoke too soon. Within days our neighbour was digging a pond and came across gravestones. He came straight round and showed us. I did some research and found there was a small cemetery attached to the smallpox one; it was for staff who had tried to care for sufferers, but contracted it themselves and died. My house, his house, the one in the middle and the two houses behind us, were all built on this cemetery! After this discovery, things intensify again.

We started asking, "Are you from the cemetery?" if we heard a noise or movement. Things intensify greatly at this point. The bathroom door starts to lock us out. There were heavy footsteps upstairs when there was no one else in. There were scrapes on the walls at night which came from the top landing. With every investigation to try to find a reasonable answer, we found nothing. It became so bad, that when my daughter came home from college, if there was no one else home, she would sit in the toilet with a carving knife until someone else came home.

Things were becoming more active now. The garden light kept being put on and my husband blamed the kids, saying he checked it at night and it wasn't a sensor light, as the switch was inside the house. The kids denied it, of course, and asked why they would put the light on while they were getting ready for school or college? This went on for months.

So, to list what was now going on: we had my daughter waking and screaming; sleep walking; things happening upstairs such as the bathroom door locking; footsteps day and night; scrapings on the walls on the upstairs landing; TVs having a life of their own; and things disappearing and sometimes not coming back for months.

My daughter wanted to swap her bedroom. She had had enough. So in 2007 the children swap rooms. Almost immediately my son is getting activity in this room; exactly the same as both his sisters previously. By now we had replaced seven TVs upstairs in four years. All of them just blew up and repairmen couldn't fix them. One night, when the children were asleep, my husband and I were watching a film in bed when we both saw a book fly off the shelf and hit the TV. Another one bites the dust, but we now had witnessed something move or fly ourselves.

We noticed that the TVs were all in the same place when they died – as did DVD players, or anything electrical. So we checked the sockets as we thought there was a chance that the socket was faulty and damaging the electrical things in that corner. This was a fruitless exercise as the socket was fine. So we decided that nothing electrical goes in that corner. We got a new TV after the book incident, and it was quite expensive and large, so we mounted it on the wall at the foot of our bed. (It survived and then we upgraded again in 2012 and that one still lives). We put nothing in the corner that had the problems now.

So, that was the first time we saw something move, but not the last. My son, Jake, was still having problems in his room with his TV, Xbox and anything electrical. He was having things taken; everything that had happened with my daughters. My daughter, who was now in the unaffected room, started to stay on and off at her boyfriend's house.

One day I was in the bedroom and cleaning her window, when behind me there was a bang. I turned around and saw that the game Cluedo was inches from the back of my feet. It had come from the top of the wardrobe. It had landed flat and the right way up, squarely behind me. There was nothing else stacked up there. It had been put securely on top. So, now a second thing had been witnessed to come squarely off the wardrobe without being tipped everywhere.

All the things that had happened previously continued as we went into 2009.

My son was having friends over to stay with us a lot. One day his friend lost his phone; it was nowhere to be found. Jake, my son, was now growing used to the weirdness, the noises, scrapes, movements and things disappearing – along with the electrical problems and the bathroom door locking him out etc. But he was worried that his friend might call him a thief. So, we rang the phone; someone answered; then hung up. We didn't hear it ring in the house anywhere, so assumed it must be somewhere else.

The friend continued to stay nearly every weekend. One night he woke Jake as the door handle to Jake's room was moving. Jake's response was, "Just ignore it, I do!" However, ignoring it was not what it wanted. We think it likes to be spoken to.

I had thought the activity had been mostly in the smaller double bedroom, both girls had been in there and now my son, and all were teenagers at the time they used it. Poltergeist activity did run through my mind, as that revolves around teenagers.

By now it was September 2009 and my daughter was off to university. Her room was stripped and wardrobes and chests of drawers emptied. The room was bare essentials, with a made up double bed, all empty of furniture and just a few odd ornaments on the shelves.

I was going up to bed earlier and watching TV up there as it felt safer, as my husband was now doing security door work and had been for a few years.

One night Jake was in his room asleep, Tony was at work and I hear footsteps in my daughter's empty room again, only this time they go on and on and I hear drawers open. Convinced we have an intruder, I grab my husband's pen knife and creep onto the landing.

The door is closed, I open it slowly; it's dark. I stand there and listen. Nothing, so I put the light on. No one is there but in the middle of the bare room is a whole bunch of carrier bags. All scrunched together and put right in the middle of the room.

The room is fairly big with an open area of carpet, no clutter. I am literally gob smacked! Where the hell had these come from? Who did it? Jake was still asleep and Tony at work. I had hoovered in there that day and they weren't there then. Why, just why?!

I came downstairs and tried to ring Tony, but the phone was dead. I looked at the socket, it was unplugged. Now panic was setting in. I was sure someone was in the house. Whose feet did I hear? Who unplugged the phone? Nothing made sense. I checked our CCTV; nothing. I put the garden lights on, nothing. I plugged the phone back in and called Tony. He said: forget it. He would be home soon. He said perhaps the cats had pulled the wire out, and found some bags we had missed in the bedroom and dragged them out. Reasonable assumption, if the cats had been in. Reasonable assumption if the phone jack didn't need squeezing to unplug. Reasonable assumption if the bedroom door had been left open and a cat run out when I went in to look. But none of the above fitted as the cats were outside!

The next night I was a little worried being alone at night, so again I went upstairs to watch TV once my son was asleep. Again I heard footsteps, scratching, all the usual stuff, but this time I smelt something. Getting out of bed, I followed it downstairs. It was gas. Every knob on the cooker had been turned on. Now they have to be pushed down and turned to let gas escape. I turned them off, opened a small window and waited for Tony to return home.

I felt as if it was stepping things up again. We now lived with TVs going on and off, lights flickering, light bulbs blowing all the time, footsteps all over the house, scratching on the walls, the garden light, things disappearing, something now jumping on all the beds, not just the one in the small double room, gas being turned on, the phone being unplugged, things being thrown off shelves, plastic bags appearing from nowhere and the bathroom locking us out.

Then my eldest daughter buys a puppy and brings him around to show us. Within minutes he is standing in the doorway barking at nothing. He wouldn't move; he was scared stiff, and shaking. My daughter left saying, "See, it's still here!" Well, we all knew that!

Shortly after that my husband was downstairs watching TV as I was watching something else upstairs. He suddenly appeared at the bedroom door, quite white. I asked, "What's up?" He replied, "I had a breath in my ear." He told me he had said, "I don't believe in you, do something in front of me. Knock on that table." He got his wish and came up to tell me. Then he told me something else that I hadn't known about.

I always fell asleep before him, and he would stay awake until the early hours. After doing door security it was a hard habit to break. At around 03.00 am on a lot of nights, he would go downstairs to double check the house was secure; on several of these occasions he had been frozen to the spot. He said that he had physically felt something come over him so he was unable to move. He would try and cling to the radiator if one was on, or grab a coat if there was time, but most of the time he would be completely disabled until it passed.

I was astounded. I had seen it happen on investigations with the paranormal team I was with; I'd seen members of the public get a physical drain, but this one was new to me. I asked him why he hadn't told me? He said he hadn't known how to explain it, it wasn't rational, he couldn't describe it and, of course, he was a sceptic too. So, I was shocked, but sort of understood why he hadn't told me, with everything else that was happening.

It had definitely upped its game since 2009 but still, we weren't afraid. Then, one night in 2010, our son came into our room and announced, "I've had a head looking at me." I asked him what he meant and he said, "It's a floating head! It's grey, it's a man and he just stared at me." I asked him if he wanted me to check it out and he said, "No, it's gone now, just thought I'd tell you I saw him." With that, he returned to his room. So, at last we knew it was a man.

So, 2010 had arrived and I decided to redecorate Jake's room as it still had his sisters' colours in there. We stripped the room and, as we lifted the bed, we found the missing phone – the one his friend had lost the year before. Its battery was now dead. But, back then when we rang it, it hadn't rung but was answered …? Jake told his friend we had found it, his friend instantly believed us as he had seen the door handle move, heard the footsteps and also witnessed the bathroom lock itself at night. He knew we were genuine.

So the game had upped again, even more. The railings and the cat incident seemed so long ago. The footsteps, noises, scratching, lighting, bathroom, plastic bags appearing, things being taken and reappearing, the smell, the gas, the garden light, the phone socket, the puppy barking, gravestones under the house, the voices in our ears, freezing my husband to the spot, the floating head, the answered phone and so much more. All were nearly everyday occurrences now.

We still stayed and again just said, 'that's it again, playing games.' We spoke to whoever this man was. We again asked for quiet nights, we asked him not to take things, or replace things which sometimes he did.

In 2011, I asked one of the paranormal team to come to my house, as it was usually more active than most of our investigations. Actually, no, it was *always* more active. So doing investigations didn't really throw up anything new to me. I had opened myself up and seen a farmer. I sensed a little boy, a farmhouse and a fire. I had sensed animals and knew when something came into a room. I wanted to do an EVP (electronic voice phenomenon) session with another investigator, to make sure it was done correctly. The other investigator was also a medium, so I knew we could deal with anything that happened.

We started to ask questions like, "Who answered Jake's friend's phone?" The answer we got meant nothing until a few hours later. The answer was "June."

We asked, "Where does Tony get frozen?" to which it replied, "At the desk and on the stairs." Both were correct answers.

We asked, "Who goes in Jakes' room?" The answer was, "Jake's people." Now this is an odd one, because this is a term Jake's grandmother would have used. Jake had lost both grandmothers within the space of ten months of each other, both Tony's and my mothers.

So we asked, "Do you live here?" to which we got "graveyard" – just the one word.

We also asked, "Who freezes Tony?" It replied, "I do," nothing else.

We then asked a few other questions like, "Who is my spirit guide?" I already knew my guide, or main guide, was called Lazarus, the answer we got was "Larry."

We then stayed quiet and just asked if there were any messages? We got the word "mum" followed by "Dennis" and then a few piano notes played.

Now Tony's mum was a singer and her partner on the piano was Dennis. Then we heard, "She is pregnant." I recognized the voice. It was my mum. I knew she meant my sister. She had been trying for years and was now thirty-two and was getting worried. We had only spoken about it a few days before.

Then it said, "Where is xxxx (my daughter)?" then it said, "Where is Jake? ... I love you all." All in all, it was a very nice, calm session. All the information was correct and recorded. It is all on the internet to hear.

After the session, I told Jake about the name we had got when we asked who had answered his friend's phone, as his friend really wanted to know. To my amazement,

June had been his grandmother's name and had died about three months before he lost the phone.

A week later, my sister phoned to tell me that she had done the test and yes – she was indeed pregnant. I didn't let on I knew; she doesn't believe in this kind of stuff anyway. We were still unaware as to who freezes Tony or walks about, but Larry did say it was him to some questions put to the recorder. But, to other questions we asked, we got the reply "I do," with no name.

After that session, life continued with its oddities, and us now saying hello to mum, Larry or June or whoever. Jake had started to "know" things before they happened. He had seen the head and he wasn't afraid.

At Lewis Road he was fourteen months old and almost two when we moved. He spoke of a previous life as a glass maker for churches back then. Perhaps one day he will develop in to medium – who knows?

Well, back to 2012. My daughter returns from university. By now we were very comfortable with whoever it is we share this house with, most of the time. We still got the footsteps, scratches, things moving, bathroom, things disappearing, TVs clicking. Nothing much had changed in the three years my daughter was away. The gas incident hadn't happened again; the phone line did a few more times, but the garden light stopped after about six months. The plastic bags had stopped, but things still came off the shelves. The noises still continued.

One night it stepped up its game again. The first thing that happened was that I was in bed watching TV, and my handbag was on the floor beside the bed. My daughter was out. Tony was playing in a band and was at a rehearsal. Jake was in his room.

The bag moved several times; I watched it with my mouth open! I shouted to Jake (now sixteen years old), and told him to check my bag as I think there is a mouse in it. He tipped all the contents out slowly, but nothing was in it. He had also seen the bag move and said, "Oh well, I guess it's a new thing!" He was right; we now started to have things in the bedroom move in front of us a lot; mostly things on the bedside tables. We could always tell when someone had come into the room as there would be a smell of perfume, or cigar, or even the smell of sweet candy floss, or I might catch a glimpse of a little light or a shadow right before the activity would start.

Tony had now started to develop his own way of protection to stop the freezing. He first used the mediumship way of mind. White light or a crystal, to working out that it needed to touch bare skin to continue, so as soon as he started to feel it approach, he used whichever method he could to avoid it.

A few days later, we were in for a BIG shock! This time, whoever was living with us wasn't just going to show his head but his whole body! The house in front of us had been burgled, and Tony and I were adjusting our CCTV. The set-up is right next to the front door, so we had the front door open, and he watched the screen as I adjusted the camera's view. Once we thought it was good enough, I went in and we watched the screen. We could see the drive, the parking area for the other two houses and up our front path.

We were quite happy with the angle, and were about to shut the front door when a whole man appeared on the screen! He was diagonal across the screen and appeared to be floating. We looked at each other, then down the path. There was no one there, yet here he was on the screen! We double checked the path and back to the screen and he had disappeared. We told our daughter what we had seen when she came home with her boyfriend.

That night they were around the side of the house, where we have a gym area. At the side gate they heard heavy footsteps getting nearer and nearer the gate. They were so loud that my daughter's boyfriend picked up a dumbbell and waited for the gate to open. It didn't. So, they opened it and no one was there. They came in and told us about it; it matched with what we had seen earlier on the CCTV screen.

Now we are in 2013, my daughter and her boyfriend move out to their own home. It is now just me, Tony and Jake, just like Lewis Road. We had now been here nine years and had got used to all the weirdness. Tony was still protecting himself from being frozen; Jake would just say, "Go away." I was back to saying, "Oh hello" or "Not tonight" or just swearing as I wasn't in the mood for searching for things or putting things back. We had become comfortable again. After all, it was nearly 2014 and we had witnessed so many things over the years, what more could it do?

2014 arrived and everything was much the same as before. We didn't see the man on CCTV again as his appearance had broken it. We installed a sensor in our big music outhouse. It had a monitor in our room so it would go off without making any sound inside the music room. We heard voices through it, but again there was no one there. The letter box started knocking, again – no one there. This continued along with everything else. But ten years on and were still comfortable.

It had all started slowly so, with so much activity over the years and the general build up, we just built up resistance too. We had become complacent about it. If something weird happened, all anyone said was, "When doesn't something weird happen here?" or "Remember we are talking about this house!" We had a very complacent attitude.

2015 came around and all that went with it. Then, the two biggest things were about to happen. It obviously didn't like us being so "whatever" about it anymore. Every year it had stepped up its game and we had adapted.

In February 2015, I was diagnosed with a type of skin

cancer. I had lesions on my ears that had to be removed. After this was done, I could not lay on my left side for sleeping. I also couldn't sleep on my back as I have spinal injuries. If I lay facing into the bed on my right side, I would get too hot. So, after the surgery I went and slept in the small double bedroom, which is now a guest room. All it contains is empty wardrobes and drawers. There is a night stand with a lamp, a TV and DVD player; all for guests. I slept there for two weeks on a specially adapted pillow. In this room I could lie on my right side and face outwards. The medication I was on was strong, so sleeping was not a problem. I always sleep with earplugs (that will explain why I didn't hear the second biggest thing in the Chaucer Way house!). It was taking time for me to heal and the tenderness to stop. I had been sleeping there now for nearly two weeks. One night I was woken by a loud bang. I turned the light on and looked about, but could see nothing wrong. Deciding it must have been Tony or Jake banging the bathroom door, I lay back down. I thought it was unusual though, as I don't normally hear anything through my earplugs, not with the drugs too. Anyway, I lay back down and went back to sleep. I was woken shortly after by very suddenly being hit in the back, legs and feet. I sprang awake and put the light on. Five DVDs were on the bed. They were all behind where my body had been, just lying on the bed. Now the empty guest room only had a few shelves with some DVDs on. There was no way I could have knocked them off; they were high up. I hadn't kicked the walls – I'm not that tall. I began to wonder about the bang earlier, so I looked down at the other side of the bed. There were two more DVDs there. Seven in total had been thrown at me in my sleep.

I picked my stuff up and ran back into mine and Tony's bedroom. I'm OK with all the weirdness while I am awake. I can deal with paranormal nights, whatever may occur and there are some stories to be told there, also. But being hit whilst asleep; that was a big no-no for me. I could cope with being walked on in the night, or something getting on the bed.

We had in fact, now seen the apparition of a grey cat, and that is what we felt was jumping on the beds. (Cat cry from 2004 solved). As cat owners we were OK with a ghost cat. I now felt sorry for the kids. If they had to go through that, and feeling now how I did, I felt awful for them. But it hadn't finished stepping up its game yet.

May 2015. At 03.00 am Tony goes downstairs, wary of being frozen, but also knowing how to deal with it. He goes to the fridge, which is at one end of the kitchen. As he opens the fridge door, a cupboard door at the other end of the kitchen, swings open. He looked up to see dishes, jugs, plates all fly out of the cupboard and smash on the floor, they flew out with such force. They flew so hard that they went of the kitchen door, and into the hallway and hit the wall at the bottom of the stairs. Loads smashed onto the kitchen floor as it is stone, and some smashed on the floor on the way to the hall. Some even smashed on the wall. The noise was huge – it even woke Jake, who does not wake easily. He ran down to see his dad open-mouthed, still standing in front of the open fridge. Jake asked, "What happened?" Of course, Tony just stood there. Jake asked again, "Dad!?" Tony told him what he had seen occur. They cleaned up and had no other choice but to return to bed.

The next morning I got up and Tony told me to watch out for the broken glass and stuff. I asked him why and he explained about what had happened during the night. I hadn't heard a thing.

If this is how my house continues now, we are ready for it. We have been here eleven years. I am thirty-two years into mediumship and the paranormal (all aspects), and we are NOT afraid. We still don't feel threatened, just aggravated at the amount of stuff that gets broken and a little peed off sometimes at the disturbances. But, if it all stopped tomorrow, the house in Chaucer Way wouldn't feel the same, and I think in a very weird and odd way, Tony, Jake and I would all miss it.

The things going on at Chaucer Way still happen to this day. Let's see what the future brings.

October 2015

This next story is also from Andrea. In this one, she tells of what happened when she went on an investigation with the rest of her team to a museum, and what they found there.

It was Saturday 14th April 2007. The paranormal team involved here I cannot name, as I no longer work with them. The investigation we were doing was at Walton Hall Museum, Stanford Le Hope, Essex, England. It is a museum of social history.

We arrived at 6.00 pm and began to set up in the areas the owners had reported activity in. They played us a recording on a small tape recorder they had left running in one of the museum buildings.

The site is used as a farm/camp/museum, but also houses a café with one connecting room that is full of social history pieces. The café has openings on both sides. It has a front entrance and patio doors at the back, which lead into a courtyard. This is surrounded by outbuildings of different sorts. There is an on-site working bakery and an old school room; children can still do art work there whilst staying at the campsite. There is a large social history building with glass cases, housing everything from old tobacco tins, old food cans, to ration books from WW2.

There is also an area which has a 'for sale' section, just a small cluttered cupboard-like area that has a treasure trove of things from the 1940s, right through to the 1980s, all which are for sale. Nothing really valuable, just nostalgic things like Etch-a-sketch, or Betamax films, rusty old Matchbox cars, old catapults, small action figures and small toys.

Also on the site is a large shed which contains old farming equipment and, finally, to complete the museum, the room connected to the café is the nursery. This room is full of old prams, dolls, children's toys all dating back from the 1930s to the 1960s. It is a treasure trove of nostalgia. There are dolls dressed in Christening gowns, some that sit watching you as you gaze around all the old prams. Some are big, some are small, and there are different materials and things hanging everywhere. They have manikins dressed as children, bed pans, high chairs adorn the walls, the floor and all around. It smells musky and feels very creepy with so many eyes watching you.

Finally in the café at the back, is a fully dressed Romany Gypsy caravan. It is fully painted, fully furnished and in great condition. All around this end are glass cabinets, with old gas masks, old irons, corkscrews, mangles and finally there is an old piano, which came from a house further up the hill when this land was a school back in the early 1900s.

The owner had inherited the museum a few years earlier from his father. The collection he had put together was his life's work. He had spent thousands of pounds collecting these items from all over the UK. He then put them on display to show the public the social history, and to educate children on how technology had changed things over time. He had done well. It was a marvellous collection and you felt privileged to be able to see and touch these things. You were able to walk among them, stroke them and feel them. Some of the collection took you straight back to childhood, or in some cases, a past life perhaps?!

The couple who now owned the farm and old school house and lots of land, along with the café and courtyard, out-buildings and farm machinery, were trying to carry on what the father had started. The old school was their private house and the rest of the museum was left for the running of campers and school trips.

However, things didn't go as planned. Once they moved in the father's old house, and re-opened the museum and camping facilities, things began to happen.

Things in their still-working bakery were being moved at night. Campers were complaining of noises coming from the museum buildings, loud crashes and bangs. Pots and pans were heard clattering around. So, the young couple left a recorder running one night and this is what they played us when we arrived.

What we heard was astounding: there was a very loud bang, then crashes, clattering and you could plainly hear things being violently thrown around. We couldn't wait to get started. There were also reports of noises in the school building, and people felt very ill when they visited the nursery.

We set up a planchette in the nursery, the kind that holds a pen and can write. We thought that being an art/school room this seemed to be the right area for it. In the bakery we set up the Ouija board, but used a glass rather than a planchette, to see if anything happened there. (Here I must stress, Ouija boards, table tipping, auto writing using a planchette holder, I am 100% against, due to the ideomotor effect. People tell us they are not moving the glass, but science tells us that this effect can happen and people can protest all they like, this ideomotor effect is real and does happen. Therefore, in my opinion, Ouija boards, table tipping, and planchette writing, is all unreliable evidence).

So, after setting up these things, plus recorders (EVPs and static cameras), we waited for the guests to arrive. As they did, they were seated at their given table in three groups. All were given a clipboard, a K2 meter and thermometer and told to take notes on any strange happenings during their vigils.

I began with a group in the café area and the other two groups were elsewhere, without a medium, as I would swap groups through the night. We did the usual things and I told the group what I was getting. Then, suddenly, the old piano played a few notes. The K2 meters started and I felt the presence of a lady approach. Every one stayed calm and we began asking questions. We asked for the K2 meter to redline for 'yes' answers and to keep it

green for 'no' or 'no reply.' This is a method I have found
to be very effective as a way of communication, mixed
with mediumship for questions, but also allows the guests
to try and use their intuition and also ask some questions.
We discovered that this lady was a piano teacher. She
appeared friendly and I did not think for one moment she
was responsible for the violent throwing of things in the
bakery. So I asked her; she confirmed it was not her, and
told us that there were four energies there. The vigil ended
quietly and politely and we thanked her. We then left the
area.

I went into the art room with the next team I had. The
planchette had hands placed upon it (not mine, may I add).
Again I told the group what I could see, feel etc. The
planchette moved slowly at first in circles. Then the K2
meters started and the movement from the planchette
became very fast and wrote, "He is coming". The group
were pretty unsettled by this. One girl felt particularly ill.
When I asked her what exactly she was feeling, she started
to cry. I took her outside and she said that she was having
flashbacks to being a child, when she was abused. This I
thought was odd, as I had picked up on children being
abused, but had said nothing to the group. We ended that
vigil, as others didn't like the way the planchette was
behaving.

The next group I had was in the bakery, the room
where the recorder had picked up most activity. We started
as normal. We had the owner of the paranormal team set a
Ouija board in there. Keep in mind that I am completely
against them, as they are in my opinion not reliable. (Today
in my own paranormal team we do not use these tools).
We started the same as always, but all I could feel was a
huge presence that kept changing its emotions. It was male
and he was limping. But that was all I said at the time. I
wanted to see what the board came up with. With fingers
on the glass, as always, it started to move in circles (as
usual, I thought: manipulation). But they had no leads

apart from a big man with a limp. So, as the glass moved faster, it began to choose random letters as is nearly always the case.

If there are no questions being asked, there will be no reaction. This continued until I said to a guest that you need to ask it questions. He asked for a name. The name Steven was spelled out. He asked the man if he lived here? It went to NO. He then asked, "Did you work here?" It went to YES. Then our K2's started flashing.

Now, in the bakery, the oven, the counter and pans are all up one end. There is a small hall with a window and then a dead end. We started to hear someone whistle and snarling sounds coming from that end. We knew it was a small passage and led nowhere; it had once housed another oven we had been told, but now was just an empty space.

As the whistling got louder, the snarling became grunts. I started to take photos to see if I could capture anything. There was blackness on the photos and nothing else. The noises continued, I put the thermal imager on and stood holding it pointing down this narrow hall.

What comes next still stays in my mind. At first, a tiny pink blob appeared. I asked it to come closer, then the pink expanded into a mass. I stood my ground and called the group. We stood and watched through the imager as the pink spread right in front of us. Then it receded until a human form appeared. There was some heat showing on the imager, but not full body heat. We looked down the hall and saw nothing, but there on the imager was a fully-formed person. I asked it to raise an arm – it did! I asked it to raise a leg – it didn't. That was when we noticed that this figure had a leg on the right side as we looked at it, but only half a leg on its left side. I asked it to sway; it did. I asked it if it could speak; nothing came.

The K2's were still flashing, so I decided to try using them to communicate. I asked it to make the K2's go red for 'yes' and to stay green for 'no.' The K2 went red. It understood. I then asked, "Are you the man I felt with the limp?" Of course it went straight to red. I asked several questions and he answered each one. I asked if he worked there, how long, in the school, was he angry etc. He answered that he had been a teacher there for thirty-five years. He walked with a cane as the war had taken his leg. Yes, he was angry at being asked to do party tricks. Then I asked some questions he wasn't keen to answer. I asked him if he was responsible for the bangs heard at night. There was a very slow reaction from green to amber, then a quick red. We find that if a spirit is not keen on a question they creep to red and only flash it. Questions they are happy with, they usually keep the meters red until we ask it to go back to green. This obviously was a question he wasn't keen to answer. I guess he knew what it was leading to. I then asked him if he had affected anyone tonight. Again a creeping red then dropping down to green without prompting.

At this point we were hearing the snarling noise again, his anger was growing; the group were afraid. I got the group leader to take them outside at this point. For the next question I just wanted me, him and one other as a witness. I asked him, "Did you abuse children? Boys?" As soon as I spoke, the K2 meters all redlined, three of them. He became very angry and I saw images in my mind no one should ever see. He backed away from the imager and was gone. The hissing and snarling noises faded. I closed the vigil and we returned to base. We had caught the image on the thermal imager on film, and had photos of it. They are still among my best photos ever.

The other groups were also back, and we told them what had happened. This place was holding demons. The recording was now explained, but still no reason as to why he was always angry and threw things. He wouldn't answer that question!

My last vigil and group was in the nursery. The group I had went ahead of me, I gave them the imager and they set themselves up in the nursery, while I attended to some distraught witnesses of the last vigil. I told the group's leader to let these people stay in the café and have a break – the café wasn't being used for the last vigil so they wouldn't interfere with anything – and she agreed.

I was making my way to my group waiting in the nursery when I got a call over the radio. It was the group's leader in the nursery. Someone had been "drained" and was on the floor. I made my way there and, as I entered, I immediately knew there were three people standing in the doorway, as I had just walked through them! The person on the floor was coming round and I ordered him out to get something sweet and not to return. (Little did I know he had attended the investigation on only three hours sleep). This is a big no-no. It makes the person an easy target for a "drain" or attachment or whatever else.

I joined the group and they had another Ouija board set up. With their fingers on the glass it moved in circles. I said what I was feeling as I always did, and the glass moved to the questions it was asked. Horrible cursing words were spelled out. I pointed the thermal imager at the doorway, and sure enough the three figures were still standing in the doorway, scaling down in size. There were two adults and a child. We tried to speak to them but there was no response. Then they disappeared, but the board continued to spell out names. We got Sarah, the word "beating" and Peter. So, armed with names, we called out to Sarah and Peter. The lights on the K2 responded. We had Peter. We asked him questions and, using my mediumship, I asked was he a former pupil, which he said he was. I asked did he know the man with the limp, and he answered yes he did. The meter started to flash like a maniac. I asked him very gently to calm down. I tried to soothe him. I asked if he was afraid of the man with the limp and he said he was. I asked Peter if the man had hurt him and he had. Peter told us that he had died at the farm in 1948. The man had beaten him to death after abusing him and Peter had said he would tell. Peter was grounded at the museum, but he also told us that so was the limping man. We asked why the man was grounded there and Peter told us that the man's wife had killed him, after she had found out he was a child abuser. She then killed herself. Asked why none of them had moved on, Peter said he was lost. But that the man and his wife weren't allowed, as the wife wouldn't allow them to. Peter said she was angry and to stay here was the man's punishment. We asked about the piano teacher and Peter said she just liked it here, so she stayed. One last question we had for Peter was why the man we thought was Steven was still angry and throwing things around in the bakery? Peter told us, via the board and the K2s, that the bakery was where he took the children with a promise of bread or cakes. Peter then told us that having living children around that he could not get at made him angry and he would throw things. We had gained so much information, it was a good investigation.

We ended that vigil and thanked Peter for all his help. We then returned to our base in the café. We spoke with the current owners and told them our findings. Then, in return, they told us that the lady who taught and played the piano, was in fact, the great-great-grandmother of the owner. It was her piano. It is always good to have your evidence verified. We asked them about a Steven who had been a teacher. They showed us a newspaper clipping about a war hero returning home and teaching at the school, he taught mechanics to boys. His name was Stephen Ferguson.

We left there, hoping to go back, but sadly it is now sold and broken up into different plots. The owners couldn't cope with the hall any longer.

This investigation is one I will never forget. Visually it is the best, but I've still had quite a few that have been more active.

I have here a short story from a lady on Facebook. I must say thanks to her as she is the first contributor from Facebook that I have had. I always said I would not go on to register with that particular method of public contact, but gave in a few weeks ago. The lady's name is Rhonda, and she would like all other details of herself and location to be kept secret. All I can tell you is she lives in Biloxi, Mississippi, and she is not part of any paranormal team as far as I am aware. So, here it is.

One night I was alone in the house and fell asleep on a couch in the living room. When I woke up, I had a rose and a note in my hand. Both of them were a neon green and glowing, and I thought my son had come home with this rose from his friend's house and given it to me with the note. He was always doing things like this. I didn't get up to read the note. I opened it and read it. It said, "You're next bitch!" I raised myself up and looked round the room. I was pissed off at this note and was looking around to see who might have given it to me.

I turned and saw a demon standing in my living room, and I threw the rose and the note up in the air, and as I did the demon ran down my hallway. We did make eye contact and I sat there trying to scream or move, but I was stuck to the couch. It took everything I had to get up and get out of the house.

I ran to a neighbour's house and banged on his door. He finally opened it and I couldn't speak. I was shaking uncontrollably and I was trying to talk but everything came out as a stutter. I finally started to calm down, due to the fact that he gave me a shot of whisky. I told him that something was in my house, and that I needed him to go and look and make sure nobody was there.

He went over to the house and looked everywhere, and came back and told me it was gone. Nothing – or nobody – was there at all. Finally, after the sun came up, I went back home and went to bed. I never found the note or the rose as proof that something was there. But this has stuck with me. I don't see things like this. I hear my name called a lot, but that's about it. So, that is my story, and I'm sticking to it!

This next story is from Beth Moore, she is with the B.A.B Paranormal team, who come from Middletown, Ohio. Again, this story request was seen on Twitter. Here is the story about Poasttown Elementary School.

It all started when I was a little girl in 1968 at the Poasttown Elementary School in Ohio. I was starting a new school. I had wonderful friends and enjoyed my four years at this school. The only thing I didn't enjoy was the creepy and uncomfortable feeling I got in certain areas of the school. Being only six to nine years old, no one ever took me seriously when I would talk about the things I felt. Every day when we would go to lunch, there was this extremely narrow hallway we would have to walk down to get into the lunch line. It was dimly lit, close quarters (even for a student) and very unsettling.

Under the stairwell that we had to line up next to was the doorway to all the pipes and plumbing to the school. I always felt like that at any moment there would be something coming out of there to scare me. There were the old heater vents that always smelt like something was burning, and a bathroom that was on the second floor that was so small, even for an elementary student, that you always felt like you were being watched by someone that wasn't really there.

The other place was out on the playground. There was a very old tree at the end of the play area. It had a hollow opening at the base of it and a very long branch that hung out over a part of the playground. My best friend Jamie and I would always call it the bad man's tree or the spooky tree. We always felt that if we played near it, we would go missing, because something would take us or, once again, that something would come out of the hollow base and scare us. That tree still stands today and has been talked about as being a spiritual portal to the other realms.

Present time, 2015. My neighbour Chrissy and I, who also

went to Poasttown as a little girl, several years after me, were talking about my up-coming paranormal investigation at Poasttown Elementary School. She then informed me of how uncomfortable the school made her feel and she proceeded to tell me about the spooky tree. I was in shock; she and I shared the same feelings and experiences at that school. Was it a coincidence? Or was it something paranormal all these years? This just made me even more excited to head off on my own investigation with my friend Shannon Griffin.

B.A.B Paranormal was created this night in August 2015. Shannon and I had both shared the same interests in the paranormal for many years. I had been investigating since 2011 and she had been on a few investigations with me. So we decided it was about time to create a team together.

It was about 9.00 pm when Daryl, the owner of the school, took us on the tour and told us the "hot spot" locations. Man, it was strange and exciting to be back in my old school! This time I was determined to get to the bottom of why I felt as I did when I was there as a child. It was personal for me – I wanted answers!

It was 10 pm when we were sent off on our own. Shannon and I bought with us, to help us investigate, her daughter, Taylor, who was thirteen; my niece, Meshayla, who was sixteen; and our friend James.

After entering many rooms that night, and having lots of rooms to investigate, and having many unexplainable events happen, we stumbled upon the special education room. Instantly I felt something different about this room. This is where we ended up spending the next two hours. Little did we know what we were in for!

It's around 1am. Shannon has her Go-Pro camera mounted to her head. We have a Laser grid, throwing out thousands of green dots over one whole wall. I am running my spirit box and digital recorder and, in the middle of this large room, there is an old school desk dating back to the

1940s. It was rectangular and could seat six students.

We were all sitting on these tiny school kids' chairs around the room. As I was looking around at the built-in metal lockers on the wall, thinking about how long it had been since I set foot in this school, I saw a large ball of light shoot across the room. That drew my eye to the Laser grid spread across the wall. Here is what we experienced for the next two hours.

We start seeing a child-sized shadow, running back and forth across the Laser grid. The set of dominoes we had set up on the small school desk in the middle of the room then falls over with no one around them, or moving near them. Taylor then feels like her hair gets pulled. This was followed by another display of this child shadow running through the green lights of the laser grid. I was getting spirit box answers left and right, with it responding to questions I asked. I thought, "Man, have we hit the room of all rooms tonight!" Little did I know that two days from that moment, I would discover the most amazing things that B.A.B paranormal has captured to this very day!

During our review of all the videos and digital recorder evidence, Shannon and I received the shock of our lives! The special education room was one very "hot spot" and this is what we found.

We captured the child-sized shadow running back and forth through the Laser grid on video; this little child also decided to show himself to us through the Go-Pro camera Shannon was wearing. There was the face of this apparition child standing about two feet in front of Shannon, watching me ask questions, then snapping his head around to look at Shannon when her Go-Pro light was blinking on and off. We then caught an EVP from this child when Taylor asked me, "When kids got in trouble at this school for pulling hair, did they run away?" We got a boy's voice in response saying, "I'm not in trouble!" During one of my spirit box sessions, I had asked, "What is your name?" We received a response not only through the spirit box, but also the Go-Pro camera saying the same name, "Tim", at two different times! We were amazed at what we had caught, but this wasn't the end yet!

When we met with a psychic medium, we told her nothing of where we were during the investigation. We only showed her our video of the face of the child apparition. She proceeded to tell us this was a little boy, his name is Tim (which name we had already caught in evidence twice). He was a fifth-grader there at the school. He loved going to that school and the year was around 1941 and that was why he is still there, because it was where he was the happiest. She said that Tim used to get "paddled" at school because he would pull Mary Anne's braids and tie them in a knot. Tim has brown hair and hazel eyes, and there are four other students there in the school with Tim.

We couldn't believe how everything tied together. It was the most fun and exciting time B.A.B Paranormal ever had whilst investigating. We can't wait to return to Poasttown Elementary School, and meet more of the apparitions that live there. If you are ever in the area, you should stop in and say "Hi" to Tim and his other friends, you will never leave disappointed!

I had just finished typing this story for you when I got a surprise! I got the next two stories from the people who went with Beth to investigate, her friend Shannon Griffin and Beth's niece Meyshala. I hope you enjoy them; it is good to have another perspective on events. This first one is from Shannon.

My journey into the paranormal began when my best friend (who I have known since 1999), Beth Moore, let me go with her to a few investigations in 2011. I would go with her to a residential house here and there, and we would catch some EVPs once in a while. Not all the time. At this time in our lives Beth was a lot more into the paranormal than I was, for sure.

In 2015 Beth invited me to go with her to Crown Point, IN. There we went and investigated the Crown Point Jail. Beth and I had got a lot of EVPs from this location, when we reviewed it. But during our investigation of the Log Room at the jail, Beth had gotten scratched. She was standing just outside of one of the jail cell doors and I was just to the left of her. It was pitch black and we were literally not able to see anything but the occasional flashlight turn on. Beth asked me to check her back, so I got my flashlight out, raised her small backpack and lifted her shirt a little bit, but there was nothing there. Maybe ten minutes go by, and she asked me again to have a look at her back, as she said it felt like it was on fire. So, I checked again and on her back was a scratch about six and a half inches long, going down. The scratch was welted like it had just happened. It looked like it scratched her upwards and the top of the scratch looked like a snake's tongue. It didn't really creep me out. I was more intrigued at that point.

From that point on, I really started getting more and more interested in the paranormal field. Shortly after our visit to the jail, Beth called me one day and said that there was an open investigation at Poasttown Elementary School in Middletown Ohio coming up. I was like, "That's maybe five minutes from my house!" Beth then proceeded to tell me that she went to that school from 1985 -1989. I became really excited about this investigation.

On this night in August, Beth and I decided to put a paranormal team together, thus becoming B.A.B Paranormal. Beth had purchased a few pieces of equipment and I had a Go-Pro camera that was not being used very much.

When we arrived at the School you could tell Beth was *extremely* excited to get back into her old school! As excited as I was to investigate! With us we had her niece, Meshayla Long, who was sixteen, and my daughter, Taylor Griffin, who was thirteen years old, and also James Wonsitler (now our cameraman).

We gathered our gear and went inside; the vibe you get when you walked into the school was just awesome! You could really tell there was something there. Then we proceeded to the break room where we met up with the caretaker of the school. What an all-round awesome guy. It was about 9.00 pm when he began to give us the tour of the school, telling us where most of the groups that come in manage to capture good evidence of the paranormal. So, with that in our minds, we decided where we wanted to go.

When we first started our investigation, we weren't really getting much in the way of responses and it was kind of hard at first to hear anything as we weren't the only group in the school, since it was open to the public for investigations on that night.

We had many experiences between the members of our group. One of which sticks out most happened when we were down in the dry storage room and the cafeteria. It was our group and another couple in the room with us. Right when you walked in it was very chilly already, but the lower level of the school was that way, so it was hard to say if it was anything for sure.

We all then proceeded to sit down in the chairs that were already there. Once settled in, Beth proceeded to ask questions. We didn't really feel much apart from being a little chilly. I was sitting in the second to last chair before you go out of the room; James was to my right, sitting next to me. He was right next to the doorway. Beth decided to turn on the spirit box (this device allows spirits to manipulate radio waves to respond to our questions). As she was asking questions, we were getting clear responses.

About twenty minutes prior to our investigation ending in that room, James, to my right, tells me that my voice recorder has stopped working. While all of this is going on, I had my Go-Pro camera mounted to my head piece. When I go to pick up my voice recorder, which was set on the ground to my right, Beth said that she had just got a major cold chill. It had been different to the chill prevalent in the room. Shortly after that we left that room and moved on to another.

Although we got a lot throughout the night, we didn't expect to catch half of what we had caught, when we went through the evidence! On reviewing the footage and recorder from the dry storage room downstairs, we had captured many EVPs, but the one piece of evidence that sticks out, was what my Go-Pro caught on video.

My Go-Pro is not night vision at all; it was pitch black, other than the green laser grid on the wall. Reviewing the footage, I got to the place where James tells me that my recorder had just stopped, so, as I panned to the right a little bit and leaned down to pick it up, little did I know that the camera on my head had picked up something amazing! There was a small, white misty cloud that moved up to my left then, a split second after, my whole screen is a misty white cloud! You can clearly see a white, somewhat small, figure rotate to the right and out the door! I have goose bumps just telling you this! Right after this evidence happened, is when you can hear Beth say, "I just got a really good cold chill." Crazy I know, but this is the stuff that is going to keep me interested for a long time coming.

B.A.B Paranormal had an awesome time at Poasttown Elementary School, and we look forward to going back as much as possible. If you are ever in the area, you should definitely stop into the School, "when you leave – you believe."

This one is from Meyshala Long, also of B.A.B Paranormal. This story is also about the school at Poasttown. It is about the Library closet.

I am sixteen years old and Poasttown Elementary was my first investigation after being asked to join B.A.B Paranormal, which was created by my aunt Beth and her best friend Shannon.

It was an eventful night, that's for sure, but the things I experienced at the School made me become a believer in the paranormal overnight!

There is one experience that sticks out the most to me. It was in the overstock room or the Library. It started when Beth, Shannon, Taylor and James and I walked into the room one by one. When I first walked in, I sat down by the only bare wall in the room, the rest containing shelves. I could feel the heaviness in the room and it felt darker than the other rooms I had visited that night in the School. I sat down in the corner closest to the shelves, with my recorder in hand. Shannon sat next to me with her Go-Pro strapped to her forehead, Taylor and James squeezed in next to us, Beth my aunt was standing up and asking questions.

In the middle of the floor we had a laser grid which was shining a thousand green dots onto the far wall. We also had a ball sitting on the floor, hoping to get a child to interact with it by rolling it or moving it.

My aunt pulls out her spirit box and starts asking questions. She doesn't get too many questions asked, when I start feeling that something other than my team members are in the room with us. I instantly had to put my head in my hands to keep from throwing up. I felt hot all over and dizzy, I started shaking uncontrollably and I didn't want to be in that room any longer. I could feel that something in there was trying to either get me out of there or attach to me. My aunt Beth noticed something was wrong with me and asked if I was all right? I explained to her what I was feeling and that I wanted to get out of there. She asked me if it was OK if she asked some questions to try and document evidence while this was happening to me. I told her that it was fine, just make it quick!

She started by saying, "Who are you? What is your name?" At that moment, our laser grid that was shining on the wall started to flicker bright and dim, like a strobe light.

She proceeded with more questions; she asked, "Is that you? Are you doing this to my niece? Are you the one making her feel sick and uncomfortable?" My aunt then asked nicely, "Please stop. She is not comfortable with what you are doing to her, please back off and leave her be."

I couldn't take it anymore and told my aunt, "Please – let's get out of this room!" We gathered up our equipment and went down into the break room. Instantly after leaving the room my symptoms went away. Crazy, I know, but trust me, everything I felt in there was real. We headed down into the break room with the caretaker of the school.

We started to listen to the digital recording from the Library closet and found out that something in there was answering the questions aunt Beth was asking! When she asked if they were doing things to me to make me feel the way I did, we had received a response of "yes," and when she asked them to stop, we got another answer, this time they responded with "no." Then as we started to leave that room, we caught an EVP of a little girl saying, "No, stay." We also caught on video a bright white orb manifesting out of the wall and heading out into the hallway immediately after Beth and I left the room.

I never truly believed in the paranormal but, after that night in August, I am a true believer now! I am very excited to be a part of the B.A.B Paranormal team, and look forward to investigating more and gathering evidence of the afterlife for many years to come.

If you would like to see and hear some of the things we caught, please visit BABparanormal.org to watch videos and hear some of the EVPs we captured at the school in Poasttown.

I have for you another story which I was given from CoPRaD, which stands for Community of Paranormal Research and Development. The story was given by James Williamson, who is a member of their team and they are based in Goodrich Texas. This is a story personal to him.

When it all started, I was about ten or eleven years old. I lived in a house my uncle had built and it was made from the remains of an old historic building. It had been the birthplace of Margot Jones (she was a theatre director and producer who lived in Texas).

At that age I never did believe in spirits and stuff, I went to church, but it was only so I could play with other children.

One morning, I got woken up because I heard voices. I thought it was just dad watching TV, so I rolled back over and went to sleep. The next night, it happened again. I got up to see what my dad was doing. When I walked down the hall, I could see that there was nobody in the living room. I even went to feel the TV to see if it had been on. It was cold; no one had been in there.

For the next few weeks it kept happening over and over again. I told my parents, but they told me it was something else, saying, "You are just hearing cars going down the road, or the neighbours playing their radio." I told them it was in the hallway to the bedroom, and it was also in my bedroom on some nights, too.

One night, I was going to prove it to them just what I was hearing. I wanted them to hear the sound of the voices talking over each other. I couldn't tell what language it was, but I could hear it was a lot of people. On some nights there was even music playing while they spoke.

So, before I even knew what an EVP was, I set up a recorder with a microphone that I had found. I waited the entire night and nothing happened. The only thing I got on the recorder was the sound of the dog!

By doing that, I must have made some of them mad, as that night was when they did the big event!

As I lay down, I couldn't hear anything, so I was pretty easy with thinking that whatever it had been had stopped. I was wrong. At exactly 3.00 am I was woken up by the voices; this time it was very loud. It was so loud that I thought it was my alarm clock/radio messing about. I was hitting buttons and switches, but couldn't get the sound to stop. I was starting to get frightened, so I actually picked up the alarm clock and threw it across the room. As it hit the ground and broke apart, it was then I realized it was not coming from the clock, but from the room itself.

I was scared and didn't know what to do, so I covered my head with the blanket. I could hear the voices talking to me through my pillow. It was then I felt something touching my foot. I assumed it was the cat whose name was Precious. When I sat up to call the cat, to come closer for some comfort, I realized the cat was not there, but something was definitely moving! As my eyes adjusted I could see what was moving up the bed: it was footprints. One step after another the footprints were walking up the bed towards my head. I quickly jumped up from the bed and left the room in a huge hurry to get my mother.

She had me lie down on the couch in the living room. Afterwards, I could still hear the voices coming from the hallway, and the bedroom. I didn't go back into the room for quite a while, and it was a long time before I heard the voices again. Sometimes, when it's very quiet and no matter where I was, I could still hear them talking, so I guess you could say that my first experience is still happening.

This next section is of interviews I have had with various people. I have found this is sometimes a better way to get the story over, as some people have said that to email the stories does feel like they are doing homework! I have to agree with them there. This way I can really get the feel of the stories they are telling me. I can also see how they react when telling them. In the last book I only had the one; I suppose I was testing the water, as they say. This time I have a few more interviews, one or two with a demonologist, and another from the TV Show co-host in my previous book. I hope you enjoy them as much as I did when I heard them.

This first one is from Brian Holloway, who is a co-host on a TV Show called 'The Ghost Trail.' The show is based in Gibraltar. He gave a story for the last book about a personal investigation he went on over a few months. This story is also a personal one which he and his wife, Giselle, conducted. The place is in Europe (a secret location), and had been used as a TB hospital, and more recently a hospital for people with mental issues. He had been trying for months, without success, to gain entry to investigate. The owner of the building always refused. Brian managed to befriend some of the Security guards, and they allowed him entry. They wanted the place investigated as they were scared to be there alone, especially at night.

Brian was over the moon, as he knew many people wanted to investigate here, and he had managed to pull it off; a once in a life time opportunity. To say he was happy about this is somewhat of an understatement. At the same time he was feeling rather scared to go in. Brian told me that this was the first time in all his investigating history (which is over many years) that he had ever felt this way about investigating a location – excitement or trepidation? The answer was: both.

The building is to be demolished shortly and apartments built on the site. After reading this account I know I wouldn't want to live there, or anywhere near it. Would you, after reading this? On talking to Brian (only three days after his investigation) he was still extremely "hyped" about what had gone on there. He apologises that the interview may not be in order of what happened, but you will shortly see why.

Brian said that he had been trying for months to get into this location in Europe to do an investigation; he was however refused by the owner of the building every time he approached them. He was not the only investigator who wanted entry, as the location had a *very* bad reputation for what was going on in there. One reason he was given was that when it was used as a mental hospital, a man had burned himself to death on one of the wards, and it was recent enough for him to still have family alive today. Brian told them he would not name the man, but was still refused.

Over the months that went by, Brian managed to make friends with some of the security guards at the hospital. He learnt from them that they were actually scared of the place themselves, especially at night when the whole atmosphere of the place changed.

One of the Security guards was a woman who Brian got to know. She told him that she was very wary of working there, due to the things that she herself had seen and heard. She told him that she was due to work a twenty-four hour shift there, and if he wanted to investigate while she was on duty at that time, she would let him do it. She told him that she would take him around and show him where the worst of the occurrences were. He had to keep it very quiet that he was going in, or she could lose her job if her bosses found out. She wanted to try and get some answers.

The security guards the company used were not strangers to danger, as many of them came from military backgrounds. This said a lot when the guards were resigning from their jobs in droves.

The first time Brian went in was at 2.00 pm, and he stayed for twelve hours. He was with his wife, Giselle, who

86

also had been on investigations with him previously. Brain said he was met by the female guard and she first took them on a tour of the building which, including the basement, was over three storeys.

Most of the building was empty, except for chairs and tables and a few odds and ends that had been left. There were long halls which had wards running off them, most being fitted out with plastic tables and chairs which were bolted to the walls, and plastic hospital beds which had been moulded into the walls so they could not be moved, for obvious reasons. All the walls were plain white tiled.

All the time they were walking around with the guard they had recorders going, and the first EVP (Electronic Voice Phenomenon) they got was in the room where the man had killed himself. The noises he got were moans and cries, the sounds of people in torment, he said.

He stressed that the building is empty and had been for years, there is no one in there except for the three of them. From now on I shall tell you the story as Brian told it to me; it is a little disjointed but he was still so excited, and he said it didn't really matter what order things happened in, as you will find out! It is better coming straight from him.

Brian says, "I have been in this place twice with my wife Giselle. We got EVPs, heard other sounds, and saw things move. This was happening from the time we set foot inside. I spoke to friends after the investigations ended, I told them when they asked what it was like, that it was fucking insane! It's a proper horror movie, scary-ass building." He says, "I was scared to go and investigate before I went in, and I never feel that way, but when I heard that a guard (who was a big burly guy) was found crying outside saying that he had seen the Devil and would never set foot in the place again, I wasn't sure if I was doing the right thing by going in myself. The guards are ex-military and hard men; this guard was one of them.

We went in anyway, and it was horrendous. We went in at 2.00 pm and the activity went on non-stop until 02.00

am. We were standing in the building thinking, 'did that just happen?' I have been in some scary-ass buildings, but this one was the worst. But I couldn't turn down the opportunity to investigate this creepy, notorious place when the chance came.

The first moans we got sounded like someone in great pain. It was in the room where the man had burned to death. I was so stunned and surprised I almost forgot to breathe. The minute you walk up to the building you know there is something so wrong; you can actually feel it giving off a feeling of 'wrongness' from outside.

When Giselle walked in (she is an extreme sensitive) she actually saw things. She was totally overwhelmed. On a normal investigation you would split the team up to see if you can capture more evidence. Here you didn't have to. It was like a roller coaster ride through a haunted house. Things were happening by the minute.

We saw big old medical beds tipped up on end, and they were as they should have been, with all four legs on the floor, when we had been through to do a sweep of the building shortly before. I moved the beds back to the way they should have been when it was a ward. They were so heavy that I had a hard time moving them! The next time we went around, they were moved again! There were chairs where there weren't any before, and I had only just left that room. I was standing, thinking, 'Am I going insane?'

It wasn't just the chairs and beds moving. There were religious statues on some of the shelves. One was turned to face the wall, so I turned it to face the room again. In the hall we found another figure. It hadn't been there before! All three of us said, 'where the hell did that come from?' It was weird.

The first time Giselle and I went in, we checked every single room in the place and knew exactly what was where. The second time we went in, there was a religious artefact that I almost tripped on. It was smashed to pieces. It was in the doorway, so I would have to step over it to get in the place.

The security staff are really that scared that they don't even bother to do the rounds properly any more. They steer clear of certain parts of the building. When people read this, they may think that as the rounds are not done thoroughly that there may be someone else there. There wasn't. People tend to stay away from the place if they have no reason to go near it. It gives off bad vibes, even from a distance.

At one point I walked down a hallway which I had been down an hour before, and there was a chair placed right in the middle. It hadn't been there before as I would have had to move it to walk around it. It was crazy, it was non-stop. I couldn't even take a break as there was so much going on.

The security guard who was taking us round, said that it got so bad that some of the security staff would go into their room, put the TV on loud and not move from there for the rest of the night.

At one point I sat down for five minutes to have something to drink, and I heard footsteps coming down the hall. I got up really quick and looked out; there was nobody there! Then I heard a door open upstairs. The noises were constant and almost pulled us around the building, following all the noises that were going on.

All the time we were there, I was constantly tripping over stuff that hadn't been there before. I actually started to really question my own sanity (which makes sense if you think that it was a mental hospital before!)

I really think that in this place, where so many people have passed over, I don't think they know they are gone.

The first night we were there, we got dozens and dozens of voices all talking over each other, all at once. The security guard with us could hear them too. We heard voices saying, 'help me,' in every way a person could ask for it. They were desperate; crying, pleading and begging.

The security guard said, "What the fuck is going on?" We were listening and you could hear a conversation going on under the pleading. One voice said, 'Do you think they can see us?' another voice answered saying, 'I'm sure they can.' The voices were constantly saying, 'Help me please! Help me please, get me out of here – help me!' That was when we heard the creepiest thing. It was a voice saying, 'It's in the basement. The darkness comes.'

The female security guard said, "Actually, at night, this place takes on a whole new feeling. It's bad and creepy." Of course the first thing I said was, "Where's the basement?" The guard told us that they didn't go down there. It was creepy in the day but at night it was terrifying; she told us the feeling was *really* bad.

Well, we did go down there and it was a proper horror basement too. I thought it was like the horror film basement where the guy at the back always gets it first! It was awful. It was like the worst basement you could imagine; from the most awful horror film you've ever seen. I went down first, then Giselle then the security guard.

At the bottom, all over the floor, were Christmas trees, and the baubles were just thrown everywhere. Further down at the end, there were statues of the Virgin Mary, Jesus and something else, and they were just staring at me. I thought, 'Yep, you couldn't make this up!'

It was a dark, dark weird place. There was a small door in the wall and behind it there was a storage space. Giselle opened the door and then jumped about a foot off the floor as she looked inside, and she let out a scream. I looked at her face and I could tell there was something really wrong. As she came out she said, "That was something I have never seen before. There was a guy, a figure, cowering in the corner, and it wasn't human." The way she described it was, "It was like Gollum from the Lord of the Rings, but uglier. It had long spindly fingers, gaunt, grey wrinkled skin and a huge pair of eyes, glaring up at me." She got out pretty quick, and all the time we were down there she kept saying to me "Don't you leave me!" everywhere we went.

The security guard said that she had heard tales of abuse of the patients, and certain other things going on, which were best left alone. You can imagine what sort of treatment went on there with the patients. I think that's why beds got moved and things got chucked about. Maybe it's because the spirits are still angry at the way they had been treated? They have to be really strong spirits to move things around like they do. This is one of the reasons that the security staff really hate being there so much.

I must admit I felt worried all the time I was there, and not just in the basement. I have never before felt *anything as bad* as this place is. I admit, I was scared. It was like waiting for something to come around the corner at you. I think the only word I can find right now is menacing. You can feel the atmosphere crushing you, your head starts to hurt and your heart races. It feels like it could burst right out of your chest as you anticipate the next thing you just *know* is going to happen! You can feel it; you can feel eyes boring into you.

The second time we went in with the security woman, there was a door they couldn't get open. She told us it couldn't be locked as the only way to do it was from a bolt on the inside, and that someone would have to be in there to bolt it. So, I went outside and looked around to see if I could find a window near the locked room. I did find one open and it was to the kitchen area, next door to the locked room. I looked in the window and thought I could probably climb in, so I did.

In the kitchen were some tables; every one of them was standing on end. So I went through the door into the room which was locked. Sure enough it was bolted shut. I opened it and went back into the hall. The guard said, "We've been in there in the past and the doors were unlocked. The next time we went to go in it was locked again. Who would do that?" I then noticed that the doors to this room were right opposite the doors that led to the basement!

So, we turned around (it was pitch black by this time but we had some torches) and saw on a toilet door handle there, a chair – a metal-framed chair – jammed onto the handle so it was sticking out vertically into the room. It looked like it was hanging in mid-air. I thought, 'Why would someone put the chair on the handle like that?' I thought, 'I have to take a photo of this!' It was just *totally* fucking weird!

We walked into the room and the guard came in with us. She said, "The room wasn't like this the last time we came in. The last time we had access to this room, everything was neat and tidy!" Now it looked like a bomb had hit it; everything was turned upside down, everything was thrown everywhere. I remember, though, at the end of the room there were some bookshelves and it was strange but every book on there was lined up in perfect order. I wondered why they had been left alone.

Thinking back on it, this was the second night, and I had taken my friend Kieran with me. As we had unlocked the double doors, Kieran said to me, "Did you hear that?" so I asked what he'd heard and he said, "It sounded like a growl and it came from the direction of the doors down to the basement." Now, I know that growling isn't usual for a 'normal' haunting. So this put us all on edge straight away. We were all still hearing the other sounds too: the cries, the sounds of someone gasping for breath – and now growling? Not normal in any way!

I haven't mentioned the gasping for breath, but it was sounding like it was very close to us. Like the people who were walking around begging for our help. There was no mistaking the noises, they were that close.

It wasn't doing the security guards' nerves any good and I was amazed at how brave she was in staying at her job. I think curiosity overrides being scared out of your wits! There are still places she won't go, though. The guards are there to stop vandalism, but the kids don't go near the place. There is not one bit of graffiti anywhere; all the kids stay well clear of the place. It feels so *wrong*.

Whilst walking around, we were monitoring and recording the whole time, and we were getting K2 hits where they shouldn't be, like right in the middle of a corridor. We were we hearing footsteps in the main area; there was no one there. We were hearing women screaming, groaning and crying out, they sounded like totally tormented souls pleading for anyone to help them, just crying out for any help anyone could offer them.

At one point in the afternoon while we were there, the security woman's boyfriend came by to check she was OK. He was amazed at all the activity we were getting, and all the things going on around us. We let him listen to some of the things we had caught on tape. We were all standing in the office at the time. He had enough when he heard a woman scream from upstairs! I asked a few questions while we were all standing there. I asked out if any of the spirits knew the name of the guard's boyfriend. A clear voice came back straight away and everyone heard it say "Ti-to." The poor guy froze. He was so shocked at hearing his name "Tito" he left in a hell of a hurry. Although, to give him his due, he did come back later that evening to check that she was still alright. She has a brave one there!

You might get one good voice on an investigation (if you're lucky!) but the voices and sounds of groaning, footsteps, and screaming just went on all the time.

I was talking to Giselle at one point and she asked the spirits to do something, and the moan we got back in response to that went on for about three or four seconds. It sounded like the person who did it was standing right next to us; it was so loud and clear, it sounded like a woman in torment and *desperate* for help. There was nothing we could see that would have made a noise like that. With an Echovox you may usually get a few noises, but this was constant, the sounds going on around us, all of the time.

When the security guard's boyfriend came back in the evening, we were listening to some of the sounds we had recorded on tape. Then, through the Echovox, we heard more talking about "the darkness comes," and the young guy was obviously feeling a bit braver than he had done earlier, as he said, "Do you mean the darkness when I turn the lights out?" and he went over and switched them off. Then a voice said, "Light on." So, he turned the light back on and his eyes were like saucers, then a voice said, "Thank you!"

Every voice we heard was clear and accurate in answering what we asked. It was totally aware of what was going on, the voice coming through the Echovox was interacting for an hour or more. Every time we asked it a question, it answered. I asked it, "How many spirits are there here?" and it gave me a number. It also started to give names! Literally it went on like this for an hour or more, answering every question intelligently. I asked where they wanted us to go and look at, and the reply we got back was, of course, "the basement."

At one point, someone suggested that perhaps we should try and arrange for an exorcism to be done, but then we agreed that as the spirits were afraid of the entity in the basement, and until we could discover exactly what it was that was down there, it would be best to leave it alone. If you decide to attack it before you can discover what it is, you could make the things going on ten times worse.

The security guard told us that one night, she was doing her rounds and walking the usual route she took, and the only thing she came across was a few chairs tipped over. She made a mental note of where they were. On her next sweep around, the chairs had been stacked one on top of the other lining the corridor. They were right next to where she would have to walk past them!

We were all having experiences like this. I was walking

around one of the rooms and there was nothing in it, but the next time I went in there, there was a figure smashed to pieces on the floor. I know it wasn't even in the room before!

Giselle went into one of the offices and all over a table in there, were keys to all the rooms. We left that office and continued our walk about. When we got back to that particular office about twenty minutes later, Giselle said, "Well, they weren't there before". There were about twelve keys that had been *placed* on the floor, right where you would walk on them to get into the office. You couldn't have avoided them. But no one had been in the room as we were all together.

By the end of the second night, I was really questioning my own sanity. I had got to know where things were and I was now pretty sure if something had been moved, or removed, since I last went in there. I doubted myself from room to room! I thought the only way to be sure was to photograph each room we went into, before we set out to do a full investigation.

Another room that stuck in my mind was the one where the guy burnt to death. The one where the table and chairs were bolted to the walls and the plastic framed bed was actually moulded into the wall. I remembered that there was a blue plastic covered mattress on the bed. I remember looking at it the first day we went in and thought it was sort of sad, and mainly because you could still see the burn marks on the table where the guy had fallen.

The second day when we went into that room, I knew something was different straight away; something was out of place and not right. That's when I noticed there was a sheet on the mattress! I *know* it hadn't been there the day before! It was perfectly made up, and tightly fitting to the mattress. The security woman said, "I can guarantee no one comes into this room *ever* because of what happened in here." So we all went in the room next to this one to see what had gone on in there, if anything. The guard said, "I am sure that is not the mattress that is on the bed in here. I'm sure it's not." The one she was looking at was a multi-coloured one; all the others were blue plastic covered ones! The guard was adamant that no one came up here. Even if they had she said, "Why would they do that? I know the other guards haven't got the balls to come up here, so who would have done it?" Again, there was no explanation for it. It was all just weird, weird stuff. To have all these things going on around you constantly, it was totally surreal.

The building is over three floors. There is the basement which is a total no-go area, the middle (ground floor), which isn't quite so bad, and is where the guards stay, and then the top floor, which is *really* creepy. On each floor there are interconnecting rooms, the place is like a maze and you lose your bearings really easily.

One time we were going round and Giselle looked into a shower room; when she came out she had a look on her face like she had had when she saw the Gollum-type creature in the basement. She said that she had just seen an old woman cowering in the corner, and the old woman had looked at her and said, 'I feel safe when she's here.' Then she just disappeared. Giselle said that she had long hair; she wasn't in the least scary. She spoke – then left! We came to the conclusion that she meant that she felt safe when the female security guard was on duty. I said to the guard, "Well, that's creepy, but it should be comforting too to know they feel safe when you're around. That means a lot." I took it that it also meant that the spirits didn't feel so safe when the male guards were on duty. I thought that might also be the reason that they were the ones who got the really bad things happen to them? We had been told stories of abuse to the patients that went on there, apparently from the male members of staff. I had heard that one of the doctors who had been there mistreated the mental patients, but that is just hearsay, although it might explain some of the feelings of fear and desperation that we were picking up on. It may also explain the sounds of moaning and pain. I reckon it must have been torture for the patients locked in there day after day.

As the place is due to be demolished soon, I asked Brian, "Where will the spirits go when it gone?" He said that he doubted they would go anywhere, and that they would stay there. I then said, "But if they build apartments on the site, what then?" Brian says that then (he thinks), the spirits would haunt the apartments and the residents would be in for one hell of time in the future! He told me that the authorities who own the property are fully aware of all the problems the building has, but they chose to ignore them. He told me that a group of the security guards went to their boss and told them that the reason guards were leaving all the time was because of the goings on there, and the reply they got was, "Don't tell anyone what is going on in there, if you do you're fired!"

Brian said, "You know it is serious when a guard turns up for work and finds the previous shift's guard outside the building and crying. When they asked 'what was the matter?' he told them 'I have just seen the Devil,' and he never went back there again. This was a big burly guy. Every single guard had, at one point, come forward to say that they had had an experience, to the point some wouldn't even bother to walk around. They all have their own ways of dealing with the place: one gets drunk and falls asleep, another turns on the TV so loud that he can't hear anything else."

Brian said that even in the middle of the day things go on. The night is worse because of the "thing" in the basement. He said, "It's weird, it's odd. You hear things that scare the shit out of you. It's not what I call waves and peaks; it is constant, every minute of every day; it is non-stop. We had electrical weirdness, where cameras would take one picture and everything was fine, the next the picture was totally black, the recorders were affected, motion sensors malfunctioned and digital recorders too."

At this point, as we were speaking, he said he had something he wanted me to listen to. He got out a recorder and pressed 'play;' I heard the saddest, loudest most anguished, moan caught as an EVP that I have *ever* heard. I felt like the person who made it *must* have been standing next to the recorder. It was as clear as someone in the room with you. The next one he played was harder to hear, but it was a woman's cry, she sounded like she was hurt and was crying out for someone to help her. It was a sad, sad sound. No one helped her then and no one could help her now. Brian told me that when they caught this moan, it actually echoed down the empty hallway. It was a cry that sounded quite simply, hopeless.

Brian apologises for all this being so disjointed, but there was so much going on that it doesn't really matter in what order he tells it. He had only investigated this building about three days before, and as you can imagine that with all he and his wife had experienced, he was still extremely excited about it. He had not had time to review everything he caught, but promises that if he gets anything else, he will get in touch, so I can let you know. All I know is that I have got to know Brian a little since he gave me the story for the last book, and the look of amazement on his face and also disbelief at how much they had come across on that investigation, I know that this story is totally TRUE. He is a serious paranormal investigator and no way would or could, have made this up.

I was trawling through the internet and decided it was time to register with Facebook, which was something I had avoided forever it seems! However, I was just looking through and seeing which people to add as a "friend" when I came across this man. I thought that as he does what he does, he may have an interesting story to share. His name is Gavin Canavan, he lives in Wicklow in Ireland and he is a Demonologist. You can contact him at Irishdemonologist@yahoo.com if you feel you could use his services, which are free of charge. His story is not what I expected.

"My name is Gavin, and I think I was born to do what I do. I got very interested in Demons when I was about ten or eleven years old. As I got older, I did a lot of studying of the subject, I then went on to work with paranormal teams and I'm a lead investigator with Paranormal Researchers Ireland, which are a scientific team, but I work outside the team doing my Demonology.

After a while I decided that Demonology was what I was most interested in, and so I began to study the subject in depth. I got some tutoring from people in this field, who were based in America, and read as much about it as I could find. I started out and over the years I have changed the way my Demonology works, and have moved more into the Roman Catholic side of teachings as a religious Demonologist. You can never stop learning. I also think that you come into your best in this field of work when you get to forty or fifty years old; the older the Demonologist the more mature and educated the Demonologist.

I charge nothing for the work I do. I get called into private homes, work spaces or where ever. What I do is clear and Bless the property, or even the person. At one point I got a call to go to Scotland, and went willingly, although it cost me a lot of money to get there. I do what I do because people need me.

When I am asked to go into a place, I go in and walk around on my own, after getting to know the people a little and putting their minds at rest. I also tell them about what I plan to do while I'm there.

On my walk through, I can get to tell what sort of presences are there, and at the same time, I call on the Angels and other spirits to protect me and the others there, the people who have contacted me.

I must stress that I do not do exorcisms. That has to be left to the Church, but I do clear the property of the Demons, and I bless the property with prayer and Holy water. I find that most of the time this is enough to get rid of anything there. I also get a Priest or Reverend in to bless the house after, and say a Mass in the house just to make sure whatever it was has gone.

The Demonic spirits have to be invited in through the occult, Ouija etc. In most cases people move into a haunted home or buy strange objects that have attachments.

There are three stages to the Demonic strategy.
Demonic infestation
Demonic infestation is when the property is haunted by inhuman Demonic spirits, their goal is to put fear into the family; the more fear, the more the Demonic will grow in strength. Everything the Demonic does is calculated; you hear a few knocks, a bad smell. Everything is done for a reason. The Demonic are fallen Angels and their main goal is to destroy us one stage at a time. When enough fear is put into a loving home, the family will start to fight with each other; their positive home turns into a negative home full of anger, hate and fear. Then the Demonic grow stronger and move onto the next stage.

Demonic oppression
Demonic oppression is where the Demonic pick one member of the family, or even all of them; they will target this person with so much force, trying to break this person down, until this person feels absolutely helpless.

Oppression is very dangerous. The person will be attacked inside their own mind with thoughts that are not theirs; they will feel and think they are going mad; they will be attacked outside their mind as well; seeing and smelling and knowing that there is something evil in their home. All your psychic senses will be on fire; your own body and soul is telling you that there is something here that shouldn't be here. The Demonic spirit during oppression, well, they break the person down; even to the point of suicide. The person might start to fall apart and turn to drink, smoking and drugs. If you can't control yourself they will control you.

Demonic possession

Demonic possession is the last stage. The Demonic can't just possess you; they need your permission. They need you to say yes. They need to break your will. God gave us all free will; we have our choices to make good or bad. When a person has been broken down, or had a nervous breakdown, this is when the Demonic possess. The person loses control and a door is open to possession.

During the oppression stage, the Demons attack with everything they have. The stronger the person; the more powerful the assaults will become. The phenomena will be tremendous in power. You will be attacked physically and psychologically. Your mind will be over-powered until you have a mental breakdown.

When a person is possessed and under the control of the Demonic, the person – or patient – appears to be invaded by new personality, a strange soul, a different ego. This alien that has taken over is hateful, aggressive, full of rage. The client's features can change; the person's voice is different and speaks in different tongues, and is fluent in all languages; especially the old languages. The body will bend in shapes that are not possible under normal circumstances; the person can levitate or see the future. The person, when possessed, can have the strength of ten humans; in most cases the client has to be tied or held down during the reading of the rite of exorcism.

There are different types of possession also.

The Lucid form of possession
During the Lucid form of possession, the person remembers everything that is happening; they are aware when the Demonic takes over and acts; they are fully conscious of switching back and forth.

Somnambulist form of possession
During this form of possession the person will have no memory when the Demonic moves into them, or takes over.

Full possession or the Perfect possession
This is where the person wants to be possessed and is happy with the Demonic possession. This can happen during occult and devil worship, Luciferians, Satanists. These people look like they are happy, perhaps married; they have kids and lead normal lives; but their eyes give them away. Their eyes look different; it's like someone else looking out. Like the old saying, "Our eyes are the window to the soul". What happens to these people when they die? Do they stay with the Demonic, or do they move into the light? No one really knows.

Now I am going to tell you the story of a family in Dublin who rang me. I asked her if I could use their story to tell you. She was fine with that but, for obvious reasons, would rather not be named.

I got to the house in question and sat down at the table with the family and talked a little to them to find out what it was they were experiencing; put their minds at rest; and tell them what I would be doing. I had two friends with me at the time who were wanting to learn about what it was that I did.

I left them talking with the family and I went off on a tour of the house. There was a real heaviness in the air.

As I walked around I started to see black shadows, in fact everyone saw them. They were very black. I blessed the whole house, room by room. I challenged whatever entities were there with Holy water and Holy objects. When you do this, it is usually the time when they come at you; that is how you can know if it's Demonic or not.

Spirits need energy, they can move objects and they can call out names. Demonic entities are fallen Angels in most cases, and they have tremendous power. They can lift really heavy objects, for instance a tumble dryer, and throw it across the room. They could kill you."

At this point, Gavin played me a tape of exactly what the woman told him about the events that led her to contact him. She sounds very matter of fact, calm. She sounds tired and accepting of events that were going on there. This is her story, which explains and sets out everything which the whole family, at one time or another, experienced.

She says, "The neighbour one night was looking out her window and saw 'something she couldn't describe' (only that it was in no way human) walking up the road past the houses.

All our things started to happen one Christmas morning. We all heard doors banging in the hall. We hear footsteps there regularly.

One night, my husband woke up and he looked down at the side of the bed, and he saw a green Goblin there. He said it had a baby's face and wings. He knows he wasn't still asleep.

My daughter was in the shower one day and she came out and showed me her back. I could see bloody scratch marks on it, with a hand print too.

We are always having pictures fly off walls or window

ledges. One day, when I was in the shower, I got a hard push. My son has heard footsteps in the house. When you are lying in bed at night, you can hear chairs scraping across the floor and noises in the kitchen. We have electrical stuff that turns on by itself.

The kids are afraid to sleep. One night my son went down to the kitchen to get a drink and he says he saw a woman sitting in one of the armchairs. Another time my son saw her; he was playing on the floor and he saw her in the armchair, but he only saw her body. He also woke up one night to see the figure of a man with long black curly hair sitting on his bed.

My youngest son is three years old. One night I went to put him to bed and there was a toy dog hanging by its neck in his room.

My brother came over at Christmas Eve and he saw the tree had been tipped over. We get rotten egg smells all through the house too.

I have never seen anything, but everything is still going on. I did do some research into the area to where the house is standing, and I did find that, when they were excavating, they found 900 or more skeletons with no heads. I suppose this might have something to do with it all."

Gavin then says, "I knew there was something upstairs, but nothing came out or challenged me. I went back downstairs and sat with the family for a while. I then decided to go back upstairs to see if anything had decided to show itself to me. I started to do a Deliverance prayer. The people downstairs said they could hear a woman screaming.

I went back down again to find out just what it was they were hearing. I knew the entity was in pain, and that it was trying to convince us all that it wasn't Demonic, but that it was a human spirit. As I then went to go back up the stairs, I got to the hallway and I heard a growl; it was coming from all around me. I heard my name shouted three times, and I also felt a gentle push a couple of times. I knew it was getting close to me. I stopped and started to pray for more protection for myself, and then I continued with the clearing.

I stayed there for the whole of the night, and at three in the morning I heard birds starting to sing outside. Birds do not break into song at that time of the morning! So then I got up and went around the house again and cleared it once more. Then the house settled down. I spoke with the family some more, as I find the more they get to know you, the more layers of their personality you get through.

It turned out that there were five houses in the neighbourhood that were infested, not just theirs. It also seemed that the other properties were having worse problems than they were. The entities were so strong.

The husband told me that when he had been in bed, the night he had seen the 'Green Goblin' creature with wings and a baby's face, the thing was beckoning him to follow it. They had spoken about it to a nun, so they phoned her and told her what had happened, and what they had going on at the house. She said that she would pray for everyone there in the house. She agreed that what he said he had found there was a Demonic little creature.

After I had been to the house, a priest came to see them the following week and performed a Mass in the house for an hour. He then went into the street and did a Mass for the whole neighbourhood, from the little green in the middle of the development. He told them all that if anyone wanted a personal blessing on their house, he would do it for them, which he did.

When I left the house, there were no more things going on there. However, when I called the family to ask if I could use their story they did say that, after the Mass had been done, one of the family wanted something from up in the attic. When they got up there, the whole place and everything in it had been smashed to pieces. I told them not to worry about that, as it is usually a sign of departure by the Demon.

It has been my experience that most Demonic happenings start around Christmas or Easter time, as these are religious times and Demons seem to love to revolt against times of the year that lend themselves to religious festivities.

Before I go to investigate a Demonic place, even before anyone has contacted me about it, I will wake up from my sleep screaming. I see things in my room with red eyes, and I am terrified. One night before I went to sleep and had a Demonic nightmare, I could hear flies buzzing in the room, and it was getting dark. I can feel the vibrations around me change. I heard a woman's voice talking to me, "Gavin, don't be afraid. Pray to the Saints and Archangel Gabriel and Archangel Michael." Straight away after I do that, the Demonic things happening to me stop.

There are not many people in Ireland who want to get involved in the Demonic side of the paranormal. I think you are born to do this work. You don't do it for money or fame. I NEVER charge for what I do. It is my calling.

Some cases of Demon activity are in fact not caused by Demons but by a mental illness, so you have to try to de-bunk as much as possible. You must treat all spirits with respect, as you do Demons. When I perform a deliverance, I do it when I'm relaxed. If I got angry and upset over what they are doing, then they have control. That is the time when you are in for a lot of trouble; the Demon can even follow you home

"I have another story which I would like to tell you about. I got a call from a paranormal team, who needed my help. A lady called Tina Barcoe, of Paranormal Researchers Ireland, called me about a family that needed help.

When we got to the house, the whole family was there. There was also the young girl, and her whole family looked worn out. They had moved house five times. The young girl actually slept in the room with her mum and dad as she was terrified to sleep alone.

She said the thing that was happening to her was that she had something talking to her all the time. It said it was going to kill her and her family. Her bedroom had been set alight twice. We were afraid that whatever it was that was doing this was really going to hurt her.

I told the family that I planned to stay with them and get to know them a bit better, and told them what I would be doing for them. I told them I wouldn't charge anything for the service I provided them and that if, at the end of it all, I couldn't help them then I would find them someone who could.

I left them all sitting down and went around the house doing a blessing. When I had finished I went back down. That was when the young girl said to me that it was telling her, 'it is going to burn him and hurt him.' So, I went through the house again and did the blessing, as I felt there might be an attachment of some type, or something negative there. I went back down the stairs again.

I walked up behind the girl and touched the back of her head with a crucifix. She jumped off the chair. I had to walk her round a few times for her to get over the shock. By this time I was starting to wonder if this was a possession? Was it Demonic? Was it an attachment? Is it an evil spirit?

I went over to the girl and I put my hands on her shoulders. In my head I was praying silently for some Angels to come forward to her and do some healing.

I then gave Tina Barcoe a piece of paper with a prayer written on it calling for the Angels to come forward, and for them to tell whatever it was we had there, that there was no reason for them to be in the house as they were dead. The Angels removed the attachment.

I must say that this is not the normal sort of thing I do, as attachments are very hard to get rid of. I rested my hands on the girl's shoulders, and could feel the energy leave while the prayers and healing were being said. The girl has slept on her own, in her own bedroom, ever since.

After about a month we went to the house again and performed another blessing. The entity/spirit had gone completely and the girl had recovered from her ordeal. I gave her a bible, rosary beads, some Holy candles and a crucifix. I get these things from church shops. I pay for them all myself. All I ever ask in payment is a cup of tea and maybe a slice of cake!

My final story for you is one about a woman who contacted me as she had two young children that kept getting scratched.

She had got a paranormal team in to investigate and they did some EVP work. They made contact with someone calling themselves James. When they played the tape back, they got a bit of a surprise as they had captured a voice saying, 'Fuck Jesus, fuck God.' I can tell you now that a normal spirit would never say anything like this.

A priest went in two days before I did and blessed the house. The family by this time were ready to believe anything they were told. I then went in a couple of days after, and spoke to the family and did a clearing on the house. I also went back a week later and did the same thing again.

While I was gone (in between visits) the family had been thinking about what had possibly caused the problems they were having. It turned out that a mirror that was hanging in their hall had been used in a Ouija board session at some point.

Every time the house was blessed, screaming could be heard coming from the mirror. You can imagine that they wanted it gone. I went collect the mirror, but when the family went to get the mirror it cracked from top to bottom. The cracks were in a zig-zag pattern. I took the mirror from the house.

I am still in touch with the family and we have become very friendly. We regularly stay in touch, and they even send me cards for birthdays and Christmas. That is the sort of payment which I am happy to accept when I help anyone out with their problems."

This next story is from a group called Chasing the Unknown and they are based in Poole in Dorset in the UK. They formed as a team about two years ago and, of course, I found them on Twitter. This team looks like it might give Culz Paranormal a run for their money with the amount of stories they have! I must say, if all the stories are as good as these, perhaps they should try writing their own book! In the meantime, I am very pleased that they have given me these for you all to read and enjoy!

The King Charles Inn, Poole was previously named The New Inn, and became a public house in 1770. The building itself can be dated to around 1550. The main part of the pub was built in the Tudor period; oriel windows and black-and-white timber-framed walls all form part of the history of the building. Once inside, you are transformed back in time; the pub still has most of its original features, with wood panelling on the walls, old roof beams and a stunning fireplace.

This is the 18th century, and the true story of a young female landlady who fell totally in love with a sailor who had to go back to sea; they promised to marry each other on his return. The sailor then went on a journey at sea for several months. When he was late coming back, the landlady assumed he had died at sea from a huge storm and, overcome with distress, she hung herself from one of the beams upstairs in her pub.

After only a few days the sailor returned, to find his love still hanging from the beam. He was so upset and heartbroken that he had pulled her down and, in despair and grief, it is said he killed himself with a knife.

On the night of October 12th 2014, Darren B, Darren K, Alison and Amy investigated the King Charles Inn. Whilst down in the cellar, Alison had a feeling of tightness around the middle of her ribcage; she described it as almost like the feeling of a corset being tightened on your back from behind. This was confirmed by Darren B, using the K2 meter going off when placed in front of Alison's ribcage, but as the K2 was moved down away from the area that the pain was felt, the K2 showed no readings. The K2 confirmed her feelings by only showing readings in the area where she experienced the pain.

After we returned from the cellar, there were several two pence coins that were placed in various areas around the upstairs of the bar (earlier in the evening) including a stack on the fireplace mantel. The only coins that had been moved were the stack, and the only way to describe what they looked like is when coins are spread out. On review of our EVPs, you can clearly hear the sound of coins tapping together.

Alison was pushed quite hard, with some force, hitting a radiator as she fell to the floor next to a table, which was directly underneath a table and chair that had been set up by the current landlords in remembrance of where the female landlady had hung herself. Alison was left with bruising down her left side of her lower back.

Amy experienced the same feeling that Alison had felt earlier in the cellar, but this was upstairs. Both Alison and Amy did an EVP session; they had direct responses to questions that were being asked by way of having the tightness around the ribcage, it tightened when the answer was YES, and each time they had the tightening sensation when the sailor was mentioned. We managed to catch an EVP of what we believe to be a young female saying, "Help me! Help me! Help me!" This was in a very quiet voice, and this was when we were asking for the female landlady to talk to us. Not long after, you can clearly hear the sound of a rope creaking.

We have lots of photos of orbs going round and round in circles, but also the landlord had a television set up downstairs, linked to the CCTV, which clearly showed the orbs moving around whilst we were investigating. We have an amazing piece of photo evidence of a male figure looking down on us from one of the roof beams. Male unknown!

Amy heard giggling, whispering and shuffling sounds from beneath the table she was sitting at with Alison. Darren B confirmed this by using the K2 meter above the table – zero readings, beneath the table – the K2 readings were going mad. Whilst Darren B was kneeling down by the table with the K2, he felt the sensation of someone rushing past him from beneath the table.

We all heard heavy footsteps going up and down the stairs but no one was there. A balloon was placed on the stairs and moved independently up and down the stairs, and was witnessed by Darren B and Darren K.

Tyneham Village is just inland from Worbarrow Bay, which is situated on the Jurassic Coastline in the Isle of Purbeck in the county of Dorset. The name of the village itself has also been known as Tiham and Tigeham throughout the centuries. This village is in the Domesday Book known as Tigeham.

On the 17th December 1943, the War Office, now known as M.O.D – Ministry of Defence, had, just 28 days prior to this date, given notice to all the villagers to temporarily evacuate their village with a promise they could return. The village was to be used to train troops for WW2. The residents were NEVER allowed to return to their homes and 'til this day the village and land is still owned, and used, by the M.O.D.

Tyneham Ghost Village, where time stood still

On approach to the village during the day time, you get a feeling of peace and tranquillity, but at night time you get this eerie feeling; hearing strange noises, a feeling of being watched, whispering and of footsteps following you and a feeling of not being welcomed.

Through several investigations, both day and night time, Darren B, Darren K, Alison and Amy captured and experienced so many varied things.

Here is our story….

Before all four of us entered the Bull house (part of Tyneham farm), we had heard several loud knocks. Once inside, Darren B asked if the Bull was present? Could he kick the floor or the wall to make a sound to confirm what we thought we had heard? We caught an EVP of the noise, which sounds like grunting and several knocks were heard after the above question was asked.

Photographic evidence shows a lot of orbs inside the Bull house around Darren B and Amy. Across the way from the Bull house were the stables; next to it was where farming machinery was stored. It was whilst we were taking pictures that a half-bodied, black figure was noticed looking out of a window. On a quick look back it had gone. We have photographic evidence to back this up.

Whilst walking around the village, Darren K was taking photos and captured a lot of orbs all around us, so the sense of being followed was backed up by what was in these photos.

In what was the Labourer's Cottage, Darren B had seen an apparition of a figure in white to his right side, near a back wall. On review of the photos you can clearly see a white figure next to him. Whilst in this Cottage, Amy heard a noise by the fireplace and, when she went to look, she was touched on her back.

In the post office, whilst Darren B was doing an EVP session, I had taken several pictures. One particular photo showed an orb above the open roof which, on a closer zoomed-in look, showed it manifesting into what looked like a dog's face. Later at home, doing thorough research, there was a picture of a black dog which sat with a nurse, Berry Driscoll, then aged 19.

Darren B and Alison were on the outside perimeter of Gwyle Cottages when Darren B saw a dark shadow figure go past the doorway. We both went inside and, using the SP11 spirit box, did an EVP session. When Darren B asked who the figure was that walked past the doorway, a mature male voice was heard saying, "Bob". Alison then asked the question, "Is anyone else here with you Bob?" A mature female voice was heard saying, "Alice". Research a few days afterwards revealed that the names Alice and Bob Wellman that had lived at Gwyle Cottages.

The Rectory was a hive of paranormal activity from the moment all four of us stepped through what was left of the front door. Darren B and Alison went towards the stables, as they had heard a noise coming from that area, whilst Darren K and Amy went to look around the other rooms inside the Rectory. Darren B and Alison had called Darren K and Amy to the stables, as they were seeing a lot of orbs, and sensing that they were being watched through a doorway. As Darren K and Amy were passing the main front door, a photo was captured of a dark figure in the doorway.

Once, all of us were together in the outside space between the Rectory, the Stable and out-buildings. Alison noticed a dark figure just showing the head, shoulders and what she could see as one hand waving at her. She quickly took pictures and managed to catch this image on one of her photos. Other pictures taken around that area also showed a tall male figure wearing a vicar's clerical collar in white, who stood next to a young child in a window, looking out towards us. Other photos show the same vicar in the doorway, and young children looking out through the windows of the stables.

In Gardener's Cottage, Darren B and Alison were doing an EVP session when they heard knocking. Darren B asked, 'If someone is here, can they knock three times like this?' (Darren knocked on the wall three times). Almost straight away, a response of three knocks was heard. This was repeated three times just to clarify, and each time the same thing happened. We also have a mesmerizing array of orbs, with some of them manifesting into faces.

Tyneham Village for us as a team has been a memorable place and one which some of us visit regularly during the day, as when you walk through the village, you feel like you're transformed back in time to the day the residents left!

Badbury Rings is an Iron Age hill fort 327 feet above sea level, made up of several barrows around the perimeter (barrows are old burial mounds). It is said Durotriges are a known Celtic tribe who built the fort.

In the 5th - 6th Century, Mount Badon, as Badbury Rings was then known, was said to be the place where a great battle had been fought with King Arthur and his army of Knights. King Arthur himself is said to have killed well over 160 men.

The story goes of noises heard at night of marching, metal swords clashing, and males shouting words in an unknown language. King Arthur and his army of Knights are said to be the ones haunting this place.

This is our story ...

We investigated this place at night; Darren B, Darren K, Alison, Amy and Mark – our newest member of the team.

The moment you walk across the last mound up to the main centre, you automatically look towards the tree line which surrounds the whole of the top centre. You instantly get the feeling of being watched by lots of people in the trees. Photographs we had taken showed dark shadows and orbs of varying colours – pink, green and white.

All five of us heard movement in the undergrowth, and as we approached a large stone with a compass point in the centre, the atmosphere around us changed to an almost intense feeling of not being welcome, and lots of faces staring at us. Lots of photos were taken around this area, showing lots of different-sized and -coloured orbs, mostly manifesting into faces; some of young children and old men.

Our equipment was set up on the main compass point, and motion sensor to the left, on a large stone plinth on the grass floor away from any of us. The sensor kept going off most of the time we were there. All five of us were stood around the centre compass at the beginning, and

116

then went off in several directions on different pathways, as lots of noises were being heard. Darren B, Darren K and Mark went off by themselves, whilst Alison and Amy went off together.

Darren B was over one side of the pond, and could see Darren K on the other side; that's when Darren B then saw what looked like a dark, full figure run across the path in front of him, towards Darren K. Darren B called Darren K to take a picture towards his direction, and the photo later showed a very large orb between the two Darrens.

When Darren B and Darren K approached the centre compass stone, they were joined by Mark, who said he saw a dark, full figure run across in front of him just after Darren B had seen it. Darren B and Amy walked away to their right of the compass point, as they thought they'd heard what sounded like laughing and giggling from a younger child! They both looked towards a skinny tree trunk, and both saw the shape of a small figure leaning against the left side of the tree. Darren B then called Alison over to take pictures. A few minutes after this, Amy felt a small hand touch the front of her stomach. When the photos were looked at later on, it showed a small dark child-like figure against the left side of the tree, and when zoomed in on the computer you could clearly see a face of a young girl.

At one point in the evening, a very strange occurrence had happened. Whilst all five of us were away from the centre point, an EVP recording picked up what sounds like a young voice saying, "Shh," and little footsteps running away from the middle. When Darren B had gone to the compass point, he noticed that one of our recorders was not there, and had shouted to each of us (Darren K, Alison, Amy, Mark) to ask if we had taken it to use. But none of us had, so a search had begun to find it. After about five minutes, Amy found the recorder turned upside down in the undergrowth, approximately ten feet away from where it originally was. On inspection by Darren B, the battery had drained by 70% but was still recording. When uploading the recording at home, the recorder was blank with no sound but the numbers were moving!!

Darren B, Darren K, Alison and Mark were standing round the compass point when Darren B felt something touch the back of his neck. Alison and Mark looked at Darren B's neck and saw three red marks. Alison then took photos as proof.

Whilst Alison was over with Amy (near to where the motion sensor was) Alison clearly saw Mark's top being held in front of him, away from his chest, and was forcefully being pulled forward, but no one was clearly seen then. Lots of photos were taken by Darren K which showed many orbs around Mark.

Later on, whilst Mark was at the centre compass point, he shouted over to Darren B and suggested using the SB11 spirit box to communicate. As Darren B walked towards the centre, he felt something hit the back of his leg and when he looked down, he saw a huge broken tree branch which none of us had seen there before.

We all decided to walk round the outside barrows and split off. Darren K and Mark on the top of the first barrow, whilst Darren B, Alison and Amy walked on the top of the second barrow. All the time we were walking, Alison was taking photos all around. Darren B and Amy saw movement on top of the third outer barrow, to the right of us. Alison took pictures, and the photo showed lots of orbs in one place on top of the mound, confirming what Darren B and Amy had seen.

All five of us joined in the dip between barrows one and two. Both Darren K and Alison were taking lots of pictures all around us an in a particular part of the dip, it felt very cold all of a sudden. Alison caught a picture of a white mist, so Darren K then took a picture in which he also captured the white mist. When looking at them at home, you can quite clearly see an outline of a person with lots of faces in the orbs all around. The coldness then left us, but we all then heard what can only be described as very loud, heavy footsteps and lots of them coming towards us, but there was nothing there. Alison took lots of pictures at that time. The photos showed over a hundred or more orbs, right in front of us, and nearly all had manifested so you can quite clearly see men's' faces in them.

At the end of the investigation, we were all around the centre compass point, packing away, when Darren B had asked on the spirit box, "Do you want us to stay?" A reply was heard saying, "No." Darren B then asked, "Do you want us to leave?" A reply was then heard saying, "Goodbye." Alison took a final photo of the rest of the team, and then we left.

A few days afterwards, when thoroughly looking through all our photos, the last photo taken clearly showed bright lights in front of Darren B on the compass stone, bright lights to his right, in front of both Amy and Darren K and, on a closer look, an unusually-shaped light on top of Mark's hand. You can see a hand attached to an arm coming from behind Mark's left side, wearing an old Victorian-style sleeve. Two heads can clearly be seen on the right side behind Mark's head, and the second looks attached to the right side of Darren B's head. Darren K has an orb on his right shoulder.

At another time, when Darren B and Alison was at Badbury Rings, they were doing EVP sessions, and it was then that Alison had her lower back touched from behind which startled her. Darren B then went off and challenged whoever was around that touched Alison, to go and touch him; and this was when Darren B was violently knocked off his feet and went flying to the ground. Alison witnessed this happening. Straight afterwards we heard banging, and the sound of marching approaching us from a distance, so we decided to leave rather quickly and whilst we were leaving the sounds got louder and louder; you could feel an unfriendly atmosphere nearby and getting closer and closer to us.

I have been given this next story from another lady I met on Facebook; her name is Karen Tammy Sandy and she lives in Champlin in Minnesota. She is retired and sent me this story which happened at her childhood home. Karen is part of the Paranormalpis Team. Another childhood story – I still wonder what makes children more prone to paranormal experiences than adults? I would love to hear your theories! My theory is their minds are not as cluttered as adults' are, as I said before.

When I was about ten or twelve years old, my family moved into a 19th Century old, spooky farm house, which had been the Poor Farm, and had also been used as a hospital and mental facility and also a nursing home in the past, but now was used as housing only.

It had a butler's pantry which had a lift that went down into the basement. In the basement there was a huge hole that had been dug but never finished. I don't know what it was for. Outside, the house had a big barn and many small buildings on the property. I think the buildings had been used for the field workers on the farm.

One day, while my mum was working in the kitchen, my sister, who was about two years old, woke up from her nap upstairs, and she started to cry. My mum asked me to go up and get her. I went upstairs and she was standing in the crib at the end facing the closet. I could see her from the hall and I went in to get her. As I did, she pointed at the open closet door and said, "Man". Needless to say, that when my feet hit that bottom stair, my sister was still in her crib! All I remember was my mum yelling at me when I ran outside!

I had seen an old man in farmer's pants and an old hat on the property too. The first time I saw him was by an old well. When I started to walk towards him – he disappeared! I saw him several times after that, but didn't make a move towards him again. The owner said that a man had died on the property, but didn't have any more information on how he had died.

121

This is a very detailed story from Ian Hughes; he is a former Paranormal Investigator, and has over thirty investigations under his belt. He says that he is very open-minded with regards to spirits, and he doesn't think every creak and bump constitute a spirit's presence. He comes from Oldham, in the UK. I enjoyed this one; it has a sense of humour too!

Drakelow Tunnels February 2011.
Drakelow Tunnels are based in Kidderminster, and over 285,000 square feet the site consists of numerous tunnels that stretch for around 3.5 miles (5.6 km), although public access on tours is limited to less than a quarter of the site.

The tunnels contained dormitories, storage areas, workshops, electrical equipment, toilets, offices, a BBC studio, a GPO Telephones communications facility and other facilities. Originally constructed for use by Rover in WWII, under the Ministry of Aircraft Productions Shadow Factory Scheme, the tunnels were mainly used for machine workshops and additional storage for Rover.

After WWII the tunnels got a second lease of life during the Cold War, where the Government took control of the site as a Regional Seat of Government (RSG), in case of a nuclear attack. Less than half the site was converted for use during the Cold War period, when new rooms and equipment were installed.

The RSG would accommodate important local and national government personnel, as well as the armed forces and a small amount of medical staff.

In the 1980s the government refurbished many parts of the nuclear site, although this was short lived as the site was sold off in the early 1990s when the Cold War had ended.

It was a very cold, yet clear, February night as we pulled up to the pretty pub for a chat with the investigation team. Sarah, the head investigator, mentioned 'no alcohol before an investigation' as a couple of students came back from the bar and sat down with their half a pint and corporation pop, and were looked at sternly. This was a rule for health and safety on site at the investigation. After the initial chat about not expecting every bump and bang to be assumed as paranormal, we all got back into our cars and made our way up a dirt path in a dark and not very well lit passageway, towards Drakelow Tunnels.

We turned into the very dimly lit car park. The trees and shrubbery from years of growth surrounded the car park lines, and gave a very surreal appearance to the start of the night's investigation.

This is where we met medium Norman Barnard, his large frame and smooth and well-groomed looks reminded me of the old days of 'Most Haunteds' Derek Acorah. We chatted for a few minutes while we waited for the rest of the groups to arrive. My then girlfriend Eliza and I walked down to the bunker entrance. The door was heavy with steel and iron and rusted with age. The caretaker opened the door, and pulled with a hefty yank.

Ahead lay a winding corridor, which was as dark as night. I quickly turned on my powerful work torch of 1 million candle light luminosity, and it pretty much paved a brightened path towards the kitchen and seating area, almost 500 yards walk ahead.

We unloaded our gear, to be met by Sarah, the lead investigator, who introduced us to the rest of the team. This was my third investigation, but as a paying member of the public. I have always been interested in the paranormal and life after death and all that comes with it, since a very early age, possibly from aged ten onwards, when I read my first book on the subject at the local library.

Here, we were split into two teams of ten people and, as we grabbed our torches to set off on the 'hunt,' we were asked to do the 'walk of fear.' Ahead of us was a pitch-black tunnel, we were asked to individually walk until we came to the broken red glowstick, and then to wait for everyone else to follow suit. My then girlfriend was a little nervous and apprehensive, and she decided to go first. Nothing of note happened to any of the group as we all walked one after the other to the glowstick, approximately 600-700 yards ahead. Then it was my turn.

I enjoy the dark, I don't mind it and have slept (due to a long day at work) on an investigation in a haunted room on my own for 2-3 hours in error. I decided to walk backwards. Nothing happened as I moonwalked my way to the group who all seemed a little shaken and nervous from the ordeal.

We came towards the old BBC broadcasting room where, should there have been a nuclear attack from Russia during the Cold War, the BBC were to be based in this office providing emergency radio broadcasts from the tunnels.

We were asked to form a circle. Now I personally do not enjoy taking part in circles, as you have to imagine a white light etc. I want things to happen, for my own sake I don't need protection. I am more frightened of being mugged in the street than demonic forces who take over your body until you leave an area etc., which I am yet to witness. I asked if I could quietly search the other broadcasting rooms, as the others in the group did their séance, and called out as per usual, asking for spirit to chat and to repeat after them like a performing dog.

1) Never mention the word spirit. If you died suddenly, then how would you know you are dead and in spirit form?

2) They are not performing monkeys or a circus act. If someone, week in week out, tried to contact me as I was dead, I would ignore them. You have to be original.

I walked into the other room and closed the door behind me. I decided to leave my torch off; white light scares the most demonic paranormal entities into thinking they are going towards the light and heaven and so dissipate, making a room turn from absolute freezing and ominous, to normal and calm.

There was an old-fashioned green dial phone on the wall; I went over to it, as you do, and lifted the receiver – there was a cackling noise on the end. It took me aback, and I immediately got goosebumps and put the receiver down. I quickly turned on my light and had a look at the cord, and followed it for a few moments until the point that shocked me: the line had already been cut! I immediately turned around and could have sworn I saw some shadow move quickly from across the other end of the room, and out through the other door. I quickly dismissed this as an optical illusion. As I was about to pick up the receiver again, the rest of the group came into the room, while two people who I didn't realize were in the room already, jumped in shock and fear. I thought to myself, I won't discuss this yet with anyone, as Eliza stood next to me and we all called out in turn, to no reply.

An hour passed, and we finished our investigation in that specific part of the tunnels, and made our way towards the kitchen and seating. Here I discussed with Eliza what had happened. She didn't believe me. I couldn't disprove her assumption either, only knowing I had had the experience.

A father and son were at the investigation, and we started talking to them. They discussed their previous experiences, and how they were drawn back again and again to Drakelow.

We finished our brews and headed out into the tunnels again. We went further into the burrows of tunnels and got told to separate into several groups of two, and each couple were placed in a tunnel. Myself and Eliza were placed in tunnel two with the father and son, the father being quite an elderly chap, with a stumpy and bald appearance, in his early 60s and equipped with a K-2 meter. His son was in his forties and a lot taller than his father. Eliza and I thought it would be funny when they called out to throw a stone. This was for our amusement, but also to see the reaction of believers and what they would do in a situation like that should anything of similar paranormal origin happen. They called out, 'Is anyone there?' I threw a small stone against the tunnel wall; they heard it and immediately said, 'Thank you spirit.' We were giggling and I threw once again as they asked yet another question. They quickly stood up and ran out of the tunnel in horror. We both tried to hold it together from laughing, and after a few minutes more of nothing happening, we were all asked to come in and stand in a circle again. I took part this time, still laughing as quietly as I could from the prank earlier.

We were all in the group holding hands; the lead investigator asked us all, one by one, to ask a question. It came to Eliza's turn, who asked, 'Do you know you're dead?' There was a huge gust of wind which blew through the tunnels with a whistle. The lead investigator asked her to call out again. 'If there is someone there …,' she said, shakily, and I could feel her palm sweating in my hand, '… can you give us a message?' There was a fairly distant crack and what sounded like a stone hit the wall behind us both. The whole group jumped; even a gentleman who was born a sceptic commented 'WTF was that?' The lead investigator then asked a few more questions to try and keep the energy going; nothing more happened for near twenty minutes, and then we were advised of another tea break.

I hate having tea breaks every hour and noticed, when we were all back in the kitchen, that Norman, Sarah's husband Jim, and Brian, were going to set up the next room a few tunnels away with a 'yes or no' game. I asked if I could tag along, as Eliza chatted to the father and son combo back at base.

We were walking in a large tunnel, Jim's red torch shone on the floor giving a dimly-lit path of red light on the floor ahead. I was at the back, fascinated. My combat pants were heavy material and I wore my Dr Martin steel toe-capped worker's boots for durability that night. I had my torch on me and, as we were walking, something clipped the side of my hip; I kind of jumped into Norman the Medium ahead of me, and quickly shone my torch behind me to the floor, half expecting a piece of cable or old copper wire protruding from the floor; this was not the case. Jim and Norman asked what had just happened, and I said I had felt something touch my hip, albeit brush past my hip. We turned off the torches and carried on walking a few paces more and I was again grabbed on my hip! I let out a 'Nooo' and a sorry yelp, and jumped into the back of Norman the Medium, checking my side as I turned on the torch. 'What happened, what happened?' the others asked.

'I have just been grabbed again,' I screeched, still in shock. 'Something tried to grab my side.'

'That would be them,' they said, with a chilling smile.

I quickly replied, as my shock turned to excitement, 'Cool ...,' whilst shouting at the cold breath I emitted in front of me, '... do it again.'

We went into what looked like an old surgery room, as the radio beeped into life and a crackle from Sarah's voice asked the boys to come back to base. Knowing where I wanted to be next, I asked if we could stay in the old surgery room, and they quickly agreed as they headed back.

I decided not to tell Eliza about the incident, and we all set off to the surgery room. I was thinking at this point what an epic experience I was having, since it was only my third investigation. I have been on many since and hardly anything happens, which is a shame, especially when you see total believers and how fake they appear on an investigation, where they 'can talk to spirit,' and communicate using their mind's eye, making things up about little demons and calling them 'squiggles.' Now, how silly is that? Seriously, and embarrassing to people who genuinely have an interest in the subject; and all the experiences through the ages that we as humans have, and the connection between life and death, and how important it was to embrace the death, as they were in the living. That was on one investigation I can always talk about another time. Back to the last part of the story.

We came to the open 50s-style doors which were on broken hinges, and made our way inside. There was another open part of the room ahead, and we walked into that area first. We had a quick look around in this room; there was a cabinet full of old consumer unit fuses, old plasters and bottles of liquids and potions from yesteryear. The glass cabinet was damaged and coated with dust of maybe fifty years or more.

The group all came in, and the lead investigator started to call out. Some gentleman, whose name I did not catch, said he heard a voice behind him. The group looked back. Myself and Eliza turned the other way, as we could feel something sinister behind us, and here we saw shine – as fast as lightning – a pair of red eyes. Eliza held on to my hand tighter as the rest of the group were having similar experiences themselves, explaining the room felt very dark, as though a blanket of pure black had been thrown on top of them. We asked again, 'Can you communicate with us?' Immediately the window pane, to our right and behind us, made a tapping noise. We decided to move quickly to the other room, trying to keep hold of hands as we walked through the broken door frame and, as we rounded each other, we were asked to close our eyes. At this point not many people I guess, wanted to do this, but I decided to.

At this point I was getting very tired, and wanted to wake up in my bed at home. As I closed my eyes, I was immediately taken back to Drakelow; but from a while back. I couldn't make out a specific moment in time, but it was like I could see what was happening in some form of time slip. As I looked over, two nurses and a military doctor and two British guards kept guard on the surgeon's room, as a patient was led inside to be operated on. The white sheet was removed and, to my horror, a being – not of this world – came into my peripheral vision. It was an experience where, for the life of me, I cannot describe the creature. I opened my eyes as a cold sweat appeared on my forehead, and something started to tap behind me. I turned around and myself, and two other people, saw a flash of a human shape with all his organs showing, which immediately vanished. We were all scared shitless at this point, pardon my language, and a couple of the girls screamed in horror as they turned their torches on, only to see on the window pane from the room we were just in, with only one entrance in or out, three distinguishable finger marks, which appeared larger at the end to the rest of the finger mark. Some say it was the mark of the Trinity. However, none of us were scratched. Personally, whatever it was, I think it was trying to show us what it had been through when the tunnels were used for military purposes.

The walkie-talkie in Jim's pocket made him jump as they were asked by Sarah to make their way back to base. We were all discussing the strange markings and raps and taps on our way back.

We got back to the kitchen, where we were thanked for the night, and walked out into the car park. The sky above was pure and glittering with millions of stars. There were no street lights to spoil the view, and the moon was a bright crisp white. Myself and Eliza got into the car and thanked everyone for an enjoyable night, and made our way home. I did get some sleep, but my experiences at Drakelow made me go back again for a second time, and again a third time.

Two years later, it turned out there was a growth of weed on the property; perhaps somehow (although I couldn't smell it), the smell or scent of the weed had hallucinogenic effects on the group – that perhaps is why I did have the experiences I did. I have not had half as good experiences as I had at Drakelow.

Perhaps one day I will go back, only I hope with a

smaller team and a whole 24 hours to investigate as much of the tunnels as possible.

This is a story from a lady who contacted me though Facebook. It is the story of a haunted object, and I believe it is the first one I have had regarding an everyday, household object. It is short but sweet, and I thank her very much for her contribution. Her name is Becky Black and she is from Michigan. She said that she is not sure how to tell it, but here goes!

I grew up knowing there was something different (about me), but things didn't really manifest until my mother and father-in-law passed away, and we inherited the house they passed away in.

So, we cleaned up the house and moved in; and instantly weird things started to happen. It only really seemed to affect me. I saw things, felt things and heard things. It was constant for me.

My husband's grandmother, who had committed suicide, had an old turkey platter that they used during the holidays. It was passed down to his mother and now he has it. I, on the other hand, absolutely hate it. It is old and ugly and I will never use it. I am always telling him, I am going to get rid of it, and he keeps saying no.

One day, we were sitting in the living room watching TV, and I hear something small fall and hit the kitchen floor. I go into the kitchen and in the middle of the floor was a small glass piggy-bank that was my daughter's, and it was broken. I looked around to see where it came from and, above my stove, the cupboard doors were wide open. Several glass items were tipped over and hanging out of the cupboard. My platters were lying down and everything was a mess! Then I saw her turkey platter; all propped up nice and neat. The strange thing is that all we heard from the living room was the little piggy-bank hitting the floor. We never heard the doors come open, the piggy-bank getting knocked off the shelf and all the glass items falling all over the place. In normal circumstances, that would have been very loud. Yet we only barely heard the one noise.

I still hate the platter and we have moved since then; it still haunts me – nothing scary – just her, making her presence known. A couple of weeks before we moved out, I had a paranormal investigation team come and investigate my home. They got several EVPs and a couple of video clips, but the thing that got me was the Ghost Box. I asked if she was mad because I wanted to get rid of her turkey platter? Plain as day, the answer I got was, "yes."

This story is from a man called Rob Hernandez, who I met through Facebook. He is the Founder and Director of the group called Pacific Coast Haunts. He is from Oxnard Beach in California. This is a story that came from the YouTube page of the Group. He felt it was too important of an experience not to let me use it here. I shall let you read it and you shall see why!

The most life-changing experience of my life, and all others who were involved, started four months ago at a house in Orange County, California. I was contacted by a client who was referred to me by a psychic who used to be in my paranormal group. The client told me she was afraid to live in her house, and was living in another property because of the events she and others were experiencing; and the fact that her husband had died in the home. Going into the investigation, I was under the impression that we were just there to cross over her husband and a lady who had died of cancer.

The moment I arrived at the home for the first time, I felt very uncomfortable, like something wasn't right. I used to be psychic and an empath, but had turned my abilities off because of spiritual attachments I used to get. Through the years I learned how to protect myself, but wasn't nearly prepared for what I was about to get myself into.

It turned out that the husband had a dark secret that was discovered after he died. I'm not going to get into details for the sake of privacy and sensitivity, but trust me when I say they were dark. We found out, much later, that he wanted to burn down the house because he knew something was there that he was protecting his wife from. He died shortly after, and the medical report said the cause was 'unknown.' It is now strongly believed that the entity in the home was what killed him.

Let me preface by saying that I wasn't the one who did the actual banishing. Their identity will remain confidential for their privacy and security, as will the other investigators and paranormal groups involved.

DISCLAIMER: the events posted are modified to shorten the timeline, although they're all presented in chronological order. All events are true and not exaggerated. EVERYONE involved with the case wound up suffering from Demonic oppression, with some suffering from illness and even possession.

Christian Apologetics and Research Ministry defines oppression as, 'Demonic oppression is the work of evil spiritual forces that urge us to sin, to deny God's Word, to feel spiritually dead, and to be in bondage to sinful things. This oppressive work is performed by Demons, which are fallen angels who resist God and who sinned in their first estate (Jude 6). They war against God, against God's people, and against unbelievers as well. Their goal is to bring as many people as possible into rebellion against God and condemnation in Hell.'

The first night I was there with another investigator, who I had only been on a few investigations with. Before the investigation began, I got up to use the restroom which is in the back part of the house. When I exited, standing only a foot or so away from me was a lady all in black, who looked exactly like the lady from the movie 'Insidious.' When you have an experience like this you can't believe what you're seeing, but both the client and the investigator saw it. I ran back into the kitchen where they were sitting, and they said my face was chalk white.

We started an EVP session while the client was there, and upon playback we got a class A EVP in my voice saying, "Who scratched me?" That was something that I never said at the time, as I hadn't been scratched. A Demon can often imitate someone's voice with perfection.

After the client left we officially started our investigation. That night, not only did we experience activity inside the house, but outside as well. We saw shadow people running back and forth in the street, and saw what looked like shooting stars coming out of the tree on the front yard (this fact becomes very significant). We also experienced disembodied sounds, voices, growls and pig grunts and oinks. We also received an EVP that said, "We've been waiting for Erik and his penis." This EVP would become of huge significance.

It was after the first night driving home, that I started experiencing things outside of the house as well. We thought we were only going to be there a few hours, but wound up leaving around 06.00 am.

Driving home on the 91 freeway with little traffic, I saw a full body apparition float in front of my windshield, from the number two lane into the number three lane. Subsequently I would get the name 'Lillith' on spirit box sessions, and every time I would get into my car the first song playing would be 'Heart of Lillith' by Inkubus Sukkubus.

We started going to the home frequently, even bringing toothbrushes, towels and a change of clothes, so that we could spend the night. Each time we were there the activity seemed to increase.

The next time we were there, I was outside smoking while the guy I was initially there with was in the main hall. The other two investigators, including the lead investigator, had gone on a food run. It was around 04.00 am. I looked in the open door of the house, and once again I saw the lady in black cross the threshold. I also saw what looked like the grim reaper, in what used to be the husband's office where certain illicit objects were found.

On the third visit, four of us spent the night. Where there should have been a wall, we captured another dimension on the FLIR. Not a portal, but an actual separate dimension. This isn't one of those cheap FLIR's you buy for the iPhone either. This was a professional model.

Where the wall should have been, was a hallway with door after door on either side, like you would see on one of those Bugs Bunny cartoons. I decided to use an invocation to stir up the energy and all hell broke loose.

Immediately afterward, on an EVP session, we got many children laughing, almost like they were mocking us. The three male investigators stayed in the living room, while the female investigator tried to go to sleep in one of the back bedrooms, which was just past the husband's office. Within only a few minutes, she came through the office, into the living room and looked right into my eyes. She said, "I will never doubt you again. I saw the hooded figure in black standing in the doorway watching over me when I tried to get to sleep." Eventually, we all went to sleep.

Everyone left very early in the morning, and it was just me and the lead investigator. Around 08.00 am he went into the back bathroom, while I lay on the couch I had slept on. Within only a few moments of him being gone, I heard, right in my ear, someone having sex and when it stopped I smelled semen. The lead investigator came into the living room and immediately asked, "What the fuck is that smell? It smells like sex." The occurrence was to be one of the most pivotal of all.

There were other times when the house was investigated, but the time before the banishing was to be the worst of all. I was not there. The lead investigator had posted on his Facebook page that he was excited about the weekend a few days before. I had asked him why and he would not tell me.

A few days later, he had told me that he and a few other investigators had gone to the house, and him and the guy I was on the initial investigation with were all in agreement that if I had gone I would have been seriously injured or even killed.

That night it was the lead investigator, the initial investigator and a female Wiccan. They did a cleansing, and were able to cross over the husband and lady who died of cancer, but something extremely evil remained.

They had a remote viewer tuned into the house, and she told them to wait until 03:15 am. At 03:17, all three of them had what was probably the worst night of their life. All three of them saw a little girl in a bathtub. The female wound up getting possessed twice, receiving over twenty bleeding scratches. She also spoke in a foreign tongue, and literally ripped off all her protective jewellery.

I won't go into any further details, based on privacy and the sensitivity of the situation. The initial investigator wound up getting extremely oppressed, screaming and cursing, which is not his nature. The lead investigator did a skrying session in the back bedroom in a tall antique mirror. He started yelling, "Fuck you! This is not your house! We're taking this fucking house back!" As soon as he finished doing that, he heard a little girl say, "Hello?" It obviously wasn't a little girl.

I talked to the lead investigator after that investigation, and he described an image he saw when he touched the lady while she was being possessed. I sent him a picture of Lillith and he said that is exactly what he saw. Other investigators had seen her through the course of four months as a hag, a beautiful lady, a little girl and the grim reaper.

Now I will tie other facts together that will prove why it is her. The first time we were there we got the EVP which said, "We've been waiting for Erik and his penis." This would foretell an event where I would wind up being sexually attacked. The semen that we smelled, we now strongly believe was actually mine.

Lillith procreated with the Demon Asmodeus to create Demon children, and it is believed she steals the semen of unmarried men to do the same. We also always saw crows flying into the tree on the front yard and leaving sacrifices. The tree itself did not look normal.

Lillith is associated with the wilderness and especially trees. In fact, one of her names is Screeching Owl. She has been seen in both her hag form and beautiful form. Lillith has both of those attributes. The lead investigator saw a vision of a wrinkled old lady with Medusa-like hair, and when I sent him the picture of Lillith she was identified.

The night after the cleansing, although I was not there, I was affected. I was on another investigation in San Juan Capistrano, and during a spirit session we were receiving responses like, "Old lady" and, "Where's my baby?" (Lillith is also known as the baby killer). When I asked if this was the old hag, all the electrical equipment went off. I was pushed out of my chair, blacked out and suffered a minor possession. It was raining outside and everyone was getting rained on when we left except me. Wherever I walked it remained dry. We knew that it was time to do something.

I personally felt a case like this was going to require more than clergy. I reached out to everyone, including metaphysical stores, initiatory orders and even secret societies. I even reached out to people who practice Goetia (Demon summoning). Nobody wanted to, or was able, to help.

Just when I exhausted all of my resources, I received an email from someone who told me they could get rid of anything, and asked if they could be of service. When I asked them later how they knew, they said they just got a feeling, so they Googled paranormal groups in Southern California and decided to click on us. You have to understand this person was born with a very special gift. When the ordeal was done, they said this was extremely challenging even for them.

Lillith is like the yin-yang. The Lillith we got rid of is the Demonic Lillith, not the Lillith that represents fertility and is celebrated at Beltane. I have worshiped that Lillith, and might even do so this May. The Lillith we were dealing with is very evil, and is one of the main Demons on the Qlipoth (the inverted Qabalah). She is referenced in Hebrew (especially the Talmud), Babylonian and Mesopotamian texts. In Hebrew, she was the first wife of Adam and refused to be subservient to him, so she tried to go to Heaven but was rebuked by Isiah, and procreated with Samael and, as referenced earlier, the Demon Asmodeus. She is also known as "the baby killer" and "La Llorona." She is often associated with the Sumerians and Annunaki as being Ninlil. She also became the serpent that tempted Eve in the Garden of Eden. I won't elaborate any further on her history, but all investigators know enough about her now to write their own book.

This past weekend is when we did the banishing. We met with the specialist, as I'll call him, beforehand and showed him some videos before going to the house.

At the house, he and the lead investigator did a walkthrough, with me in tow. He could actually see her and chased her through the house with a big smile on his face saying, "There you are." He was able to trap her in the mirror, where we had earlier done the skrying. He had blocked me for my own protection, so I didn't experience anything, but both he and the lead investigator said that things were crazy. He did a few things to the mirror, and placed a few things on it before doing a final meditation to bind her and whatever else was left, but I'm not going to go into any of the details. However, doing this oneself can lead to possession, serious injury, or even death.

The specialist left, and the lead investigator and I spent the night. We did not notice any paranormal activity like we usually would, until I went to sleep. I had extreme nightmares, out-of-body experiences and found out I was sleepwalking.

In the morning, the lead investigator went to go use the restroom (which is near the back bedroom where the covered mirror was). He heard a voice say something like, "Let me out of the mirror. Let me out." Both he and I were tempted to lift what was covering the mirror, but decided against it. Instead we duct-taped it, and put it in the back of his car. We had taken an amulet off the mirror and were outside smoking. He said he was going to leave it for the client and I asked him if that was a good idea. I said, "It might be charged with her energy." As soon as I said that I got extremely dizzy and fell down hard. Although I landed in some dry bark, it was hard enough and with enough force to possibly give me a concussion. If I had fallen only a few inches further over I could have been killed, as there was a concrete brick on the ground.

Later that day I had a call back for an audition. The casting director asked me what the craziest experience I ever had was, and obviously I told her this, being much more severe than the skeleton arm that attacked me. When I told her this, I started shaking and actually broke down crying on camera. She told me I was brave and thanked me for my courage.

I found out later that the day, that around the same time I started crying, the lead investigator had gotten rid of the mirror and had an emotional situation himself. There have been many offers to buy the mirror but he is not going to sell it, no matter the price. In fact, a friend of mine wanted it to use for an extreme horror simulation that he runs. Whenever I ask about the mirror I'm just told that it's gone. My belief is that if, it were found, it would be more dangerous than other haunted objects, such as Robert the Doll or even Annabelle.

This situation to me is one of, if not the, most important cases in paranormal history. By getting rid of the Demon Lillith, biblical history was literally made. I'm glad I'm not the one who actually did the banishing because, however evil she is, I don't feel it's my responsibility to play God. This situation could have had global ramifications, and although I'm told she is forever gone, I believe that Demons never disappear, and that there's a slight possibility there still could be here.

Though, after thirteen years, the client finally has her health, sanity and home back.

I'm not very religious, but I recently saw a priest who prayed for, and with, me. He also blessed me with holy water. When he was saying his prayer, we both heard a disembodied bell sound. There were no other people around and no reason to hear that sound. The bell represents Sanctus.

This is from a group called ParaskeptiX. They are based in Arizona, you may be able to tell from their name what they are and you would be right. The group try to expose the fakery that goes on in the paranormal investigation world. They have had some 'run ins' with some very big names in the field of paranormal investigating and, as such, are not particularly popular with some of them. However, it is always good to check out both sides of the coin, so to speak. I found this group on Twitter and these stories are from one of their members, C.H. Considering what they do, you can be assured these are most certainly TRUE!

This took place in a home in Nashville, NC, beginning in 2001. My mom and I lived in the home while my father was working in another state until he could transfer.

We started noticing a porcelain doll of a man on the mantle would be turned around backwards every time my father would leave the home. My mother thought I was doing it and I thought she was doing it. It started to happen so often that my mother moved the dolls off the mantle.

At different times there would be the smell of coal in the house, or we could smell perfume, like it was moving through the home. We could hear footsteps; the front porch swing would swing on its own. My parent's bedroom door would close on its own, even though the house had settled, so that the door should have swung open instead.

There was a time when my mother was sitting in a chair in the living room and saw the reflection of a woman walk in front of her in the window, but there was no one there.

My father was locked out of the house one time. I had an experience where I was sitting in the kitchen one night on the computer, when I got the impression that someone was watching me from behind. The feeling got so strong that I decided to go to bed. As I walked out of the kitchen I saw a black mass reflected in the mirror opposite the doorway to the kitchen behind me.

One day, as I was getting out of the shower in the hallway bathroom, I saw just an arm going into one of the bedrooms off of the hallway. Just an arm, swinging like someone was walking in there. A couple weeks later, my girlfriend – who is now my wife – was brushing her teeth in the same bathroom, and called me to come stand with her while she was in there. I asked why and she began describing seeing the exact thing I had seen, with the arm going into a bedroom, but I had not told her about it, and she is a non-believer in ghosts.

Multiple visitors to the home would mention seeing something moving past the doors to the bedrooms in the hallway. On the night of my wife's high school graduation, my mother had a medical emergency earlier that day and I had to go home and get my father some clothes to spend the night in the hospital. When I went home, I could feel a heaviness in the house. I got what I needed to get, and I cut the light off in the hallway as I was leaving. When I got to the kitchen door I said, "Alright I'm gone," and the exact light I had cut off switched back on.

One morning, when my father was getting ready to go to work, he noticed the cat asleep on the floor in front of him. He got up and walked into the kitchen, when the dog outside went crazy. He opened the door to see what it was, and the same cat that had been asleep thirty seconds ago in the bedroom, ran into the house from outside, with no windows or doors being open.

My brother is former military, and was at the house with me one night to take care of our parent's dog. I left him in the house and a few minutes later, he busted out the door screaming. A shadow that wasn't his was watching him in the hallway mirror, and turned its head to look at him when he noticed it. I have other stories from this place, but that should do it.

ParaskeptiX decided to let us have a bit more information about the house above, and sent this for everyone to enjoy; short but sweet, I would say.

There was one evening when I got hit one night lying in bed. I was sitting in bed and something hit me in the side of my knee. My shoe rocked heel to toe on the floor one night beside my bed.

My oldest daughter was three at the time, and she was spending the night with my parents. She was in their room with them, when she said she wanted something to drink. My mother told her to go get something from the fridge, and my daughter stopped in the hallway and ran back and jumped on their bed. When my mother asked what was wrong, she said there was a woman with red hair standing in the hallway. My mom said, "She's a nice lady, just say hello," and began saying hello to the 'woman.' My daughter got scared and climbed under the covers, and my mom asked why, and my daughter said the woman had come into the bedroom.

My oldest daughter also had an incident over there, where she was sitting on the porch swing with my mom and dad, when she said, "Grandma, I don't want to go and sit on his lap," and was pointing at the chair across the porch when no one was there.

My mother was doing laundry on the porch one night, and turned to find an old woman leaning out of the doorway watching her. My wife and I stayed with my parents for a while after we got married to save some money and, on the last night there, all we had left in the bedroom was the mattress we were sleeping on. Again, my wife is a sceptic and didn't believe in ghosts, but she said she woke up, and could see the outline of a woman standing beside the mattress looking at her.

My father was recently back in the area on business, and saw the woman outside that had bought the house from them. He stopped and asked if they had anything happen, and said the woman turned pale, and said that her son had been telling her and her husband that he was seeing someone in the house, but they thought he just had an imaginary friend.

The house was built in 1910 and, while we were living there, we had noticed that the living room was always pitch black, even though there were three windows in the room and the house sat on the corner next to a street light. One time, an older lady, who lived down the street, was walking by and my father talked to her about the house, and she commented that they had always talked about the house being haunted, even when she was younger, when they would walk by the house going to school.

This story has been given to me by a lady called Susanna Savidge. I again found her on Twitter and she was most pleased to give this for you. She is from Texas and is the founder of Texas Paranormal Investigators. She tells us -

My first paranormal experience happened in the house I grew up in on Zelda Street in Hurst, Texas. My parents bought the house in 1970, the year before I was born. My parents later divorced when I was seventeen, and I stayed in the house with my mother who was disabled.

Nothing unusual ever happened while I was growing up. I had the normal, occasional nightmare that would lead me to getting into my parent's bed for comfort.

In 1999, I remember clearly that I was laying on my right side in bed, trying to go to sleep. I remember the feeling of a presence start to lie on top of me. It started as a gradual motion, moving from my feet and traveling up my body. The pressure was not even as heavy as a small child, or animal, nor was it cumbersome. It was a smooth, gliding motion. I must have been aware of it right before, or the second it started, because I remember pulling the covers up over my head, squeezing my eyes as tight as I could and yelling in my mind, "Help me Jesus!" As soon as I prayed for help, it lifted straight off of me. It was not a gradual recession. It was a quick, even lifting off. The whole event could not have lasted more than a few seconds. I do not believe that this was a case of sleep paralysis. I did not have any of the common symptoms of sleep paralysis. I was able to move. I did not feel like I was being held down, choked or suffocated in anyway.

About this same time, my mother encountered the black shadow figure with the wide-brimmed hat. It came to her at night in her bedroom. She saw him on two different occasions. She said that the feeling she got was one of pure evil. She said that her room never felt the same after that first encounter with it.

Later that same year, my mother went into the hospital

for a total knee replacement. Since she was going to be gone for a week, I decided I would brighten her room by giving it a coat of fresh paint. I was alone in the house while she was gone. I went to work, came home, and went to sleep without any issues. However, when I started to prep the walls of her room for painting, I would get the most unnerving feeling of being watched. No matter how hard I tried to ignore it, I would end up just leaving the room. What should have taken a couple of days ended up taking the whole week!

We continued to live in the house until 2005, when my mother went to live in an assisted living facility. I then sold the house. The last six years that I lived there, the whole house had a dark aura around it.

To this day, I have no idea what it was or, how it came to be in our house. My mother and I are both Christians and have never dabbled in the occult. I have always wondered about the folks that have lived in the house since I sold it. I certainly hope that whatever that was there left the house after it was sold and never returns!

This story is from Austin Green, who is a part of The Ghost Watch team. I found this team on Twitter. They are a new group from Michigan USA. They also have a YouTube channel and include video clips on Ghosts, Aliens and Cryptids, you might want to give it a watch!

My story comes from the Soop Cemetery off Old Denton Rd. in Belleville MI, behind the I-94 Service Drive. The cemetery has many tombstones from the 1800s and many ghostly tales. I live about half an hour away, so I visit it on occasion. I used to be a part of a paranormal investigative crew, since disbanded, and we did an investigation of Soop cemetery.

I decided to wander off to the other side of the cemetery. I was using my camera to hopefully pick something up – and I did: two pairs of glowing red eyes in the distance. When I zoomed in, it looked like human outlines around the eyes, although that might be a trick of the eyes. This was no reflective surface or animal.

There is a yellow reflective sign on the other side, and the eyes are above the tombstones, but below the tree branches. That means they are hovering, and you could tell if it was an insect, bird, or bat.

Later on, a couple of the investigators who are sensitive to the paranormal sensed a little girl and, when we put our hands where she was supposedly standing, the temperature was colder than the air around us.

Another time, my mother and I visited the cemetery at night, just to do a quick investigation. I pulled out my recorder and started asking questions. As soon as we started asking questions I heard something run up to my side although I could see nothing there, and we also heard knocking on the surrounding trees.

Another quick story I have is from Forest Park off I-75 in Lincoln Park, MI.

A few days before Halloween 2015, me and my friends, James and Ray (we are trying to form a paranormal group) decided to do a little investigation. I did not think anything was going to happen, but we heard some weird sounds, such as knocks on trees, which may be animals, but also some EVPs. I caught a scream on my recorder, that I did not hear normally, and Ray and James claim they heard someone say "Hey!"

We were not that far off from a neighbourhood, but we never heard the scream, and I never heard the "Hey!" and I was standing right next to them. I do not know if there are any stories from Forest Park, but it is kind of eerie at night.

This next story is from Eddie from Blacklight UCD. They are based in Ontario in Canada. I contacted this group on Twitter and they are very pleased to be able to send stories for this edition. They have a YouTube channel you may want to check out too. After reading this story I think it may get loads of views! They also investigate UFO's for MUFON and Cryptids. Let's see what you think of this offering!

My name is Eddie Berdan, born in Barrie, Ontario, Canada in 1972. In order for you to know the full story, I need to tell you all where my story begins. This is only one of the lifetime of stories and events that I have to share and, let me tell you, my stories would terrify most of you to live even one of them.

I have had a dark entity attached to me for forty-two years, and have spent many years researching and investigating the events of my life, to pin point where it all started. Still, to this day, it remains with me wherever I go.

Let me dive in. Not long after I was born, my parents loaded my sister and I and all of our things up, and set out for Surrey, B.C., Canada. We moved into the house; that would be where my story began. At the tender age of ten months old, I had a double hernia and as a result almost died, and from that moment on things in my life got pretty nuts.

How many people can say they remember the smallest details from a place they lived in at ten months old? I can, and I have talked to my father of it at great length. He is absolutely floored that I can remember anything, let alone most everything, right down to the layout of the house and events that happened in it. Keep in mind we are talking 1973 and have no pictures for me to have gotten the information from.

Now I skip ahead to the story at hand. It begins as our family relocates yet again, this time to Winnipeg, Manitoba, Canada; the month is October 1980. We are just moving into our new home. It was new to us, just a rental but it was to become home. We lived in this house until June of 1984, and I would say the longest we ever lived at one address.

The activity started almost immediately after we moved in, and got worse as time went on. They say that paranormal activities can cause high EMF readings and in turn, make people sick or angry, and even make them act like someone they are not.

All of the above started happening as soon as we moved into this home. I was eight years old; having dreams so violent that I would be punching and kicking holes in the wall while I slept, and not feeling a thing. Also, I was always sick with something: a cold, an ear infection, chicken pox, the measles (two or three different types I might add).

Along with the anger and sickness, constantly, the activity in the house got worse as time went on. You could hear someone walking up and down the basement stairs, then the door opening and closing again. All night, every night you would hear this, along with things moving when no one was up to move them.

In 1982 my dad bought a pinball machine for the basement for all of us to play with. One more thing to make noise as we slept; the machine would play by itself, you could hear the ball rolling up and down the deck and the bells going off. It was crazy so we unplugged it, and still all night it would be playing away, and in the morning it was still unplugged.

One night, I gathered up the nerve to go down and peek my head in to see if it was on. Sure enough, I peek my head around the corner and all the lights were on, bells going off. As I took one step closer, the stairs creaked and everything went dark, and the noise stopped. I got my ass out of there in a hurry.

It was July 1983 when I would get my first and only glimpse of the dark entity that has been attacking me all of my life. It was that one event that scared me so bad as a child, it changed me to the core.

I got up that evening; everyone else was in bed asleep. I had to use the washroom, but felt extremely uneasy – more so than usual. Like I was being watched and someone was there. I got up, turned on the lamp in my room as I did not want to be in the dark.

I got up, went to the washroom, and barely made it; by this time I was freaking out. I ran back to my room and turned my clock radio around so I could see the time. It was 3:05 am and I was terrified. I jumped back in bed, and heard footsteps coming toward my room.

We had hardwood floors throughout the living room and my bedroom. I was shaking, so I pulled the covers over my head. It was a knitted blanket so I could still see through it. Here comes this dark mass that looked to me like a huge dark man all in black; and I could not see a face, like he did not have one. The fear in that moment! He looked to have an axe or something in his hands. It scared me so bad as he stood next to my bed.

I literally passed out from fear. As I woke in the morning at 5:30 am, I uncovered my head, as it was still covered. I thought, "Wow that's some crazy dream," and gave a sigh of relief. Then I noticed my lamp was still on, and my clock radio was still turned. It gets worse: the clock was stopped at 3:05 am. My heart started pounding, but it was light out as it was the summer, so I go to get out of bed. Things got weird as I went to put my feet on the floor; I saw something on the floor so I got down to have a look.

There was a heel print of a very large boot embedded into the floor. It was like it was burnt right into the hardwood floor; right where the figure was standing. Let me tell you, I got my clothes and got the hell out of that house that morning. That was when I knew it was not a dream; it did in fact happen, like many of the other events it was real.

That was the first, and the last, time I actually saw the

dark entity. Many others have seen it throughout my life, in every place I have lived. To this day it will not show itself to me. Instead it lurks around, attacking me; trying to hurt me or scare me; trying to wear me down, for whatever reason. I am not scared easily these days; not much scares me at all. That clock radio never worked again!!!

I presently work with Blacklight Investigation Uncharted Division; investigating the paranormal and trying to help others deal with their paranormal issues.

This is a story from a new ghost hunting team called MR Ghost Hunters. They are a three person team and this is the story from Matt, who is the Co-founder. It is about Annesley Old Church in Nottingham where the team are based. The Church is very old and is built on the Chaworth Estate, and lies two miles from the Byron Estate. In 1765 the 5th Lord Byron killed William Chaworth in a duel.

I found the Team on Twitter and they consist of Rich the founder, Matt the co-founder and Sharon who is the researcher/manager. Annesley Old Church is now a ruin.

We did an investigation at Annesley Old Church. We have been a few times and got some responses, but the last time we went, it felt heavy all around us and you could feel things near you, but couldn't see anything. We wanted to go and investigate because we had heard so many claims of paranormal things, like screaming, stones thrown, black figures and a woman in a window of Annesley Hall, which is just next to the church.

So, we went on to Annesley Old Church grounds, and as soon as we walked on, our team had a weird feeling; like being watched, followed and even something sneaking up on us, but as soon as we turned our torches on, we couldn't see anything. We decided to start filming on our camcorders. So, we walked straight across to the church tower. We did an EVP, and a few voices came through, but we couldn't make out what they were saying.

We saw black shadows moving around, so we had a walk around and still couldn't see anything, so we stopped at a wall next to Annesley Hall and did an EVP, but nothing came through. Rich saw something over our guest (K's) shoulder, so we went into that direction, and again didn't find anything.

We felt like they were playing games with us, so we decided to go to Mary Ann Chaworth's grave where we did a SB-11 spirit box session. As soon as Rich turned it on, a woman's voice came through and said, "It's cold." So, we carried on with our session, asking all sorts of questions. We had a name come through, "Byron," which made perfect sense, due to the history of Lord Byron. Mary Ann was Lord Byron's childhood love, and Lord Byron was buried somewhere in the church grounds.

We got a bit excited, and carried on with our session, and had a woman came through, who said Sharon's name, and said, "It's cold." Sharon replied saying, "I'll help you," and the spirit responded back saying, "No, you can't."

Then, all of a sudden, we got a really heavy feeling that they were all around us.

I (Matt) had something run up behind me and tap my back; so straight away, Rich did a quick EVP burst session, in which Rich asked, "Who ran up on Matt and touched him?" We had a quiet voice say, "Mary." Then Sharon heard voices; as soon as she heard it, Sharon grabbed her phone to take pictures but it died straight away, even though it was fully charged.

Straight after that our guest, (K), was grabbed on her arm, but we couldn't see anything, so we decided as a team to take (K) back to the car. She was a little bit spooked, and Rich and I left Sharon at Mary Ann's grave, with a cam and a torch.

As soon as Rich and I got to the car, I got a bad feeling, so we went back to collect Sharon. She told me how she heard walking and voices through the SB-11. Someone told her to 'Shut up!' so she left and something was thrown at her, but she couldn't find the source, and she was also being told not to leave. I decided with Rich that this was the best time to leave, which we did.

This story comes from William Payne who lives in Indiana, USA. I contacted him again through Twitter. He is a paranormal investigator and also a Demonologist. Oh, and in his other life he is a musician. Enjoy his story.

When I was younger we came home from vacation from Florida to find our house burnt to the ground. Apparently we had a bad storm and lightning went right through the middle and caught it on fire.

We got it rebuilt, but something didn't feel right. At night I would be awakened by sounds in the halls and even saw a full bodied apparition. It was of a woman of African descent. She wore the clothes of a female slave.

After that things would start moving, and we had one lamp that would randomly turn on no matter where we put it. I had a friend stay one night, and we stayed in one of the spare bedrooms. The door to the room slammed shut on us and we couldn't open it. It didn't have a knob so it should have opened.

I was afraid of what was going on, and no one believed me. After some time my uncle and his family moved in with us, after he was medically discharged from the Army. It was him, his wife, and their two kids. The youngest stayed in my room. He was one year old and I was fourteen at this time. After some time, the baby was acting strange. He started to have a very mean attitude, one no child at this age should have.

He would claw at us, scream and spit. We thought it was just normal behaviour for a child even though none of us ever did that. We knew something was wrong when everyone in the house was awakened by him. I was awoken by a voice in my room, my aunt and uncle heard it through the baby monitor. He came into the room while his wife got my grandparents. Their baby boy was speaking Latin.

That is when my grandmother called her old Priest and had him visit. He came and interviewed us, and found out that while we were at Church, my aunt would stay home and play with a Ouija board. We blamed his possession on this. We all had to take part in an exorcism on my cousin. Afterwards, he blessed the house and my aunt burned the Ouija board, which I now know isn't the best thing to do.

After that I started to learn everything I could about the paranormal, and have even taken Demonology classes through the Old Catholic Church, so I can help families understand if a family member is possessed, or just suffering from an over-stressed mental breakdown, which is usually the case now. I haven't had to deal with anything Demonic since then and pray that I never will ever again. I hope nobody in this line of work with the paranormal will ever have to deal with a Demon.

I received this story from William Jacquin; he followed me on Twitter and thought he would like to share his story with you. He did supply a couple of brilliant pictures to go with it, but unfortunately they can't be reproduced here. This, however, does not affect the story in any way, so enjoy it.

On Feb 8th 2016 I visited Dresden, Germany with my wife and two of her co-workers. One of them, being from Dresden, became our unofficial tour guide for the day. It was fairly quiet in the city; not many tourists around at all.

So, around five in the evening we walked into the Stallhof, which is a part of the castle complex where they held jousting tournaments in medieval times. It was completely empty except for the four of us. As her co-worker explained some of the history to us, I took a picture, walked a few steps and took a second picture.

After about fifteen minutes we left without anything strange occurring. Later on, in my hotel room, as I looked through my pictures I spotted something I couldn't believe. Two milk-white figures with all black clothing on. A female figure stands holding her coat or scarf with one hand, and a white purse in the other. Directly to her right is a man wearing an officer's hat and holding something that appears like a book, he's looking towards her. I also noticed in the first photo it looks as though they're forming: her torso floats in the tunnel area, with purse, as two dark shadows of the same shape form in between her and him. The dark shape where she ends up standing in the second picture looks like it's quite possibly showing ectoplasm.

The Stallhof was damaged badly during the bombing of Dresden in February of 1945 but rebuilt later.

I had nearly completed all the stories and interviews from all the contributors, when I got a message from Eddie (who also supplied a story a little earlier). He said he had another story for us; I had to include it here. It would drive most of you crazy I think! Perhaps he should get in touch with Gavin who also supplied some stories here a little earlier? I can quite see how it took him ages to write. It is very disturbing.

I am Eddie Berdan. I am 43 from Barrie, Ontario, Canada. I work with Blacklight Investigation Uncharted Division. I want to call this story 'An Attack On My Mind, Body And Senses.' It's a true story.

Have you ever felt like you were not alone? Like you had someone watching you? Felt a hand touch you when you were all alone and laugh it off as being all in your head? There was a time where I thought I was just super-sensitive; having gut feelings and having all of the hair standing up on my arms and neck. I always knew something out of the ordinary was taking place in my life.

After all, how likely would it be that every place I can ever remember living in would have paranormal activities? I mean every one; with the altered emotions of anger, fear, sadness. There were always unexplainable things happening. From the noises of people walking around when no one is there, to things being moved or knocked down or even hidden, only to find them months later right where you left them.

It all seemed harmless – even playful – at times. As a child it scared me like crazy, but as I got older it was interesting and sort of funny for the most part. The activity was worse at times than others. It almost seemed to stop at times for a month or two, only to come back worse each time. Like it was stepping up its game with every return; or powering up?

Returning each time, getting bolder and more scary.

It is hard enough to live with for most people, but even harder when you live with something you can't see or hear.

As I said, I had no reason to feel threatened or fearful for many years. It was like living with Casper the friendly mischievous ghost. Then things started to get strange and much worse.

Having unexplained bruises or scratches just appear out of nowhere. Waking up in a cold sweat, not being able to move a muscle or even make a sound. Waking up with injuries you had no way to explain. It happened more and more as the time went on.

Then, once again, the activity seemed to just stop for a couple of months; absolutely nothing. We are talking a lifetime of activities; which at the time of this was well over thirty years. So things went quiet and all was good – or so it seemed.

It was the fall of 2006, my ex-wife, our four-month-old puppy, my ex's brother and I lived in a basement apartment in Bradford, Ontario. Things were pretty tight there, so we decided to find a bigger place and it just so happened some really good friends of ours just bought a house that had a 3 bedroom upper, and one bedroom lower unit. So we decided it would be a great time to make the move as it meant more room for all of us, and it would help a good friend. Win-win, or so we thought.

We got ourselves moved in and settled and almost immediately things started happening yet again; but this time things were different. Our puppy, Raven, would go nuts barking at the stairs up to our bedrooms where the washroom was. He would not go up there for anything when this was going on. The noises got louder and more often. Things would be thrown instead of just being knocked down. This went on for months, taking us through the winter.

It was the spring of 2007 when things seemed quiet for a couple of weeks, so we thought, as usual, we could breathe easy and relax a bit and start to enjoy our new place. We were nearing summer; it was getting warmer and the outside was not the only thing heating up. The activity started yet again this time getting downright nuts; scary even. The dog was losing his mind.

So, things came to a startling head one day when I came home from work. It was a hot summer day; I just finished working, all sweaty from delivering a truck load of metals, as I was a truck driver.

I got home, nobody was there except Raven; the ex-wife and brother-in-law were at work. I go in the house take off my boots and put away my lunch bag and stuff. Things just felt odd and heavy right from the moment I opened the door.

I did things as usual, and tried to ignore this feeling of fear that seemed to be consuming me. Raven was standing at the bottom of the stairs just going completely nuts, and that just added to that fear and uneasy feeling. The tension in the air was so thick you could almost taste it.

I go upstairs, grab a clean change of clothes and my towel, and get undressed ready to wash this day and all of these feelings off me. I could not shake the feeling that I was not alone. I mean, it was intense. So, I go into the washroom and though I was alone and the only one in the house, I felt I needed to lock the door behind me. Raven, still at the bottom of the stairs, barking his head off and cowering around the corner.

I started the shower, put my clothes on the vanity and hung my towel on the towel rack, across from the vanity. It was a rather large bathroom; you walk in and there was a double vanity on a wall, across from it a towel rack, then past that the toilet and the tub and shower across from that.

I got in the shower as I always did, started doing my thing letting the hot water run over me trying to relax. Then I lather up, rinse off and proceed to wash my hair, water beating off my back; and that's when things got serious and downright scary.

Rinsing my hair, soap in my eyes and something grabs me. I don't mean a touch; I mean it grabbed me – lifted me five or six feet off the ground and turned me a complete 180 degrees – and dropped me on the floor.

I landed on my back between the vanity and the wall with the towel rack on it. I never hit a thing in the room, nor did I even hit the shower curtain. I was facing the opposite way that I was standing in the shower, on my back, naked and totally freaked out.

I could feel hands grab me and pick me up and throw me. I am a big guy – 6'1 and 240lbs – and, whatever it was man-handled me, I was helpless to do a thing. I could not see anything doing this, or even grab a towel on the rack or the curtain on the way out. I landed perfectly straight; not hitting a thing. Never had I felt more powerless and bewildered.

That was the first of many violent attacks on me, and I wish I could say that it was the worst. Unfortunately, many other attacks have happened since, and at least one was more violent and terrifying.

It is hard enough being attacked by things we see and can fight off or defend against; nothing harder than trying to explain these events to someone who was not there, without sounding absolutely nuts. This is the life I live and, unfortunately, the activity and attacks continue to this day. I only pray no one else has to go through what I have, and still do, go through.

EWB

This is a story from a lady called Catherine Lee Holderby, aka ParanormalPosion. At the time she was living in Loveland Ohio, but now she is in Maryland. I met her on Facebook and this is one I hope gets you thinking! I know it would have worried me!

When this Paranormal Experience took place I was the only child left at home, I was 14-15 years old. This particular event I believe stems from many.

My father became friends with a man that did a sort of Paranormal Radio Show in Cincinnati, Ohio back in the 1970s. This man became a frequent visitor about every weekend in our home. He was there to entertain, if you will, my parents and a few of their friends. Paranormal experiences began happening on a regular basis.

I was awakened in the middle of the night, I do not know by what, but I am awake in a total dark room, when I hear this chilling voice breaking the silence in the house by calling my name. Too afraid to move, I did the classic thing and hid under the covers. I was thinking I would pass 'The Voice' in the dark if I tried to get out of my bedroom. However that did not last long, for as soon as 'The Voice' sounded again, I was gone, down to the living room!

Still shaking, I turned the living room lights on and lay down on the couch. After a while of silence, I began to calm down and get sleepy again. Getting comfortable, I turned to face the back of the couch. Nice and comfy, ready for some shut-eye.

That was when I begin to hear faint footsteps on the hardwood floors. It sounds like from the hallway; mom or dad must be up. I listen as the footsteps get louder, approaching me, then passing and heading for the kitchen. No need to look, its mom or dad, I will pretend to be asleep. If they see I am awake I will be told to go back to bed.

I begin to hear the footsteps leaving the kitchen. Although something is different this time, they seem louder while still at a distance. Are they walking harder, upset? Oh no, maybe they wanted that last piece of cake I ate! As I hear them get closer and much louder, I begin to feel uneasy; it's as if they are stomping. I'm really not going to look now! I almost want to scream, when the footsteps stop! There was complete and eerie total silence.

Now, you would think that would be a good thing. No, not for me; that's when every hair on my body stood to attention and this chill started at my head, sweeping down my whole body. For you see, the footsteps ceased right at the couch by me!

I jerked around to look, all the while praying, please let it be mom or dad! When I opened my eyes what I saw in front of me was – air, absolutely nothing. Surprised I could even move, I ran to my parent's bedroom door and, upon planning on enjoying the rest of night there, propped against their door, I turned the bathroom light on leaving the door open.

At this point, feeling as though I had drank a pot of coffee, my mind was racing. Replaying the night and listening for any sound, while praying for the sun to rise. Funny now, how at that time I was thinking I would never forget that night, for I didn't know yet what still was in store for me.

I was a nervous wreck and constantly looking all around for any movement. I took a glance in the bathroom. I noticed very small drip in the sink; it was easily viewed from my position on the floor.

Now, I can't tell you why I began focusing on this small drip. Maybe it was soothing at first, or just something to do. But for whatever reason it seemed to have helped calm me. No more voices calling my name in the dark, I hadn't heard anymore invisible stomping footsteps for a bit.

Just in a kinda relaxed state, watching this small drip in the bathroom sink. Then I noticed this drip was not so small anymore; not sure when it got bigger though. I was thinking dad wasn't going to be happy he had to fix it, when the drip became a small steady stream. OK, now I am back on alert, what the heck? Am I imagining all this stuff? Bull, I'm just not going to watch the drip anymore. I decide I will close my eyes and sing to myself, in my head of course, so I can still listen for any strange sounds. I close my eyes and begin my song; that's when the faucet turned on full force!!

I did not go in the bathroom and turn it off, for I did not see who turned it on. Instead, I jumped to my feet and began yelling and pounding on my parent's door. They always kept their bedroom door locked, or I would have already been in there. By now you could safely say I was close to hysterical!

When the door opened I ran in, giving them an account of the night thus far. I was given a pillow and blanket, which I used to nestle myself on the floor by the closet facing the open side.

Lying there I said a few prayers, wiping my tears away. I was thinking maybe to make some sort of sense of this all come morning.

You know that feeling you get when someone is staring at you? I was getting that feeling and like something was telling me to open my eyes. So, I open my eyes, looking into the closet. What a mistake!! For there, staring back at me was this, THING.

I'm not really sure how long I actually looked at it, but its image is forever etched in my mind. You do not see something like this and forget it. This thing was staring and eerily smiling at me; it couldn't have been over two feet tall.

In describing what texture its skin may have been, I would say reptile; rough with ugly bumps and visual veins. The colour looked to be a dirty greenish-black, with a dirty yellow tint. The large ears appeared further up on head and had a rounded point; the edges of the ears were very veiny. Just an ugly face, fat scrunched-up nose and dirty yellow-brown broken teeth. The eyes were coal black, beady; a look that makes you nauseous.

Breaking the shock, trance or whatever, I let out this bloodcurdling scream and landed right between my parents.

I continued sleeping with them until they had a priest perform an 'Exorcism' on our home in Loveland. Oh – I would like to mention that this "Thing" was seen by others over those years of paranormal activity in our home. I had never seen anything like it before, or since.

So reader – that is the final story for you. I do hope that they were an enjoyable experience!

As I promised you at the start, I have asked someone who is a sceptic of all things paranormal to give their view on what has been submitted.

Their comments are not directed at anyone, or any one story in particular, and by no means are they meant to cause offence. It is just their sceptical views.

If you are reading this, I hope like me you are also believers, but I also think that there are two sides to every coin, and everyone deserves a say on what they think is plausible, or not.

Having said that, I just need to thank everyone again for the time and effort to those who gave these for you and I have also put a list of acknowledgements on the last page. A very big thanks also goes to you for reading this.

I am now off on my next literary undertaking, as I have been asked to write the story of how CULZ PARANORMAL were formed and to give their stories for you to enjoy. Keep an eye on Twitter and Facebook, I will be sure to let you know when it's coming out!

SCEPTIC'S COMMENT

When I was first asked to review and comment on the stories within this book, I had planned to add comments after each story. But as I began to read the stories, I was struck with how personal some of the accounts were. I then began to feel bad about adding comments to these; it felt disrespectful to those people who had shared something that personal. So I decided to write my comments here at the end of the book instead. As I said at the start of the book, these are just my thoughts and ramblings, please don't take offence.

Reading this collection of stories I find it fascinating that so many people jump to similar conclusions when confronted with a noise they can't identify. People have an ingrained need to believe in something, especially when they are grieving for a loved one, any noise or bump in the dark must be dear Uncle Bob trying to communicate from the other side. They never seem to consider that there might be some rational explanation.

Several of the stories in this book fall into this category and as such, I find it hard to place a real faith in them. Could they be just natural noises that people attribute to the supernatural just to satisfy their own needs?

This then brings me to the next type of story. Those people who seek out the supernatural experience. It is well understood that the subconscious mind likes to be proved right, and will fabricate and influence the conscious mind to achieve this. What is sometimes referred to as 'wishful thinking.'

How many of these experiences are actually the subconscious mind inventing experiences just to satisfy the need to be right? Over the years there have been many experiments in and around the power of suggestion. If you tell someone that if they go to a specific location they will experience something, how many times will that actually happen? To me several of these stories in the book have a ring of suggestion to me.

If we are to believe that people are experiencing contact from the other side, then we should consider what it is they might be experiencing.

If you believe in the after-life, then you most probably believe in some form of Heaven and Hell. By definition, Heaven is meant to be a really cool place, so why would anyone hang around here or want to come back? They wouldn't. Likewise, Hell is meant to be really bad and run by that Devil bloke, I really can't imagine he would be too pleased to leave his guests here, or have them popping back for a chat.

I find it hard to believe that we really do get contact from the after-life.

I have heard many different explanations for what ghosts or spirits are, and have yet to hear one that to me stands up as plausible.

Now we come to the stories from the Demon hunters. These stories are intriguing; they open up an interesting line of thought.

If you consider the possibility of other realms, call them Heaven and Hell, the earlier creations of God, or even Hinduism's Moksha and Samsara (although these are not strictly Heaven and Hell, you get my meaning) then you have concede that there is the possibility that within these realms there are entities or beings. Now, if there are, and they have found a way to be able to cross over to our existence, it opens up a world of possibilities. Could this be what people are experiencing, both the Demon hunter and the Ghost hunter?

Although there are many interesting stories within this book, personally, I don't think there is enough to alleviate all my doubts or scepticism. They do raise some interesting questions and I would love to have the opportunity to speak directly to some of the people who have shared their stories. I am also sure that, should I one day experience first-hand what some people have written about, I would quickly change my view – that, and be running for the hills!

In closing, I would like to thank all the people for sharing their stories and to thank Erica for giving me the opportunity to read and comment on them. Hopefully my comments and ramblings have not upset too many people and that you have found them of interest.

ACKNOWLEDGEMENTS

P.Act Paranormal North Carolina	@PactParanormal1	Twitter
Ghost Cr3w Lynchburg Virginia	@THEGHOSTCR3W	Twitter
UK Shadow Seekers Manchester	@UKShadowSeekers	Twitter
Nocturnal Visions Paranormal Tennessee	@NVP152	Twitter
Anke Caver Germany	@anke_carver	Twitter
Tony Parkes Devon	@tpslumia	Twitter
Culz Paranormal Colorado	@Therealculz	Twitter, FB & YT
Andrea Halford Dartford	@ajhalford42	Twitter
Rhonda		Facebook

BAB Paranormal Ohio	@babparanormal	Twitter
CoPrad Texas	@coprad_com	Twitter
Brian Holloway Gibraltar	@TheBigB1969	Twitter, FB & YT
Gavin Canavan Ireland	@gavedemonologist	Twitter FB
Chasing the Unknown Dorset	@UnknownChasing	Twitter, FB
Karen Tammy Sandy Minnesota		Facebook
Ian Hughes Oldham		Twitter
Becky Black		Facebook
Rob Hernandez California		Facebook
ParaskeptiX Arizona	@ParaskeptiX	Twitter
Susanna Savidge Texas		Facebook

The Ghost Watch Michigan	@TheGhostWatch	Twitter YT
Eddie Berdan Ontario	@theraven72	Twitter, FB & YT
MR Ghost Hunters		Facebook
Catherine Lee Holderby		
William Payne		
William Jacquin		

WITH HEARTFELT THANKS TO YOU ALL –
I COULDN'T HAVE DONE IT WITHOUT YOU!

www.ingramcontent.com/pod-product-compliance
Lightning Source LLC
La Vergne TN
LVHW051408080426
835508LV00022B/2994